JOHN DEWEY

The School and Society

Edited by Jo Ann Boydston

With a Preface by Joe R. Burnett

SOUTHERN ILLINOIS UNIVERSITY PRESS

Carbondale and Edwardsville

FEFFER & SIMONS, INC.

London and Amsterdam

Arcturus Books Edition, August 1980

Printed by offset lithography in the United States
of America

The text of this reprinting is an exact photo-offset
reprint of Chapter 1 of the original cloth edition of
Volume 1 of *The Middle Works of John Dewey,
1899–1924*, edited by Jo Ann Boydston, which con-
tains the full apparatus for the volume awarded the
seal of the Center for Editions of American Authors
of the Modern Language Association. No changes
have been made in the text.

Library of Congress Cataloging in Publication Data

Dewey, John, 1859–1952.
    The school and society.

    (Arcturus paperbacks; AB 151)
    "First selection in volume 1 of John Dewey: The
middle works, 1899–1924."
    Includes index.
    1. Dewey, John, 1859–1952. 2. Education—
Philosophy. 3. Educational sociology. I. Boydston,
Jo Ann, 1924–   II. Dewey, John, 1859–1952. The
middle works, 1899–1924. III. Title.
LB875.D4 1980   370.1   79-26919
ISBN 0-8093-0967-X

PREFACE

This slight volume began inauspiciously from three talks which Dewey gave to parents and students at the University of Chicago Laboratory School in 1896. To transcriptions of these talks other writings were added to produce the first published edition in 1899.[1] Roughly 3,000,000 copies of *The School and Society* have now appeared, and laudatory references to it are very common in the recent literature on education—interestingly, some of it literature representing very diverse, often-conflicting political and philosophic positions.

There are many reasons for the work's popularity for well over half a century. Perhaps one that is less obvious than others is that during this century we have been working out the educational problems which were being "set" in the late 1800s. To some of these problems the volume is a very coherent response; viz., those arising from America's unique emergence from an agrarian society into one predicated on massive industrialization, ever-and-ever-more sophisticated science and technology to drive industrialization, unchecked and largely unplanned urbanization to concentrate worker-citizens in the small geographical productive regions demanded by industrialization, vast international involvements, and population (including immigration) surges.

The other side of the Janus face of these trends was the demise of the extended family and communal neighborhood village in agrarian society as sources of human emotional security, stable community- and family-based child-rearing practices, economic and political autonomy, and largely unchallenged religious orthodoxy.

1. A second edition, consisting of the deletion of a few essays and substitution of others, was produced in 1915. A third edition did not appear until 1956 when the University of Chicago Press joined the work with another of Dewey's educational classics, *The Child and the Curriculum* (first published in 1902), in a single volume.

The volume is something of a "patchwork" response to the problems, given its mode of creation, but at least five main themes clearly and importantly are discernible in it. The first of these is that industrialization, urbanization, science, and technology have created a revolution never "in all history so rapid, so extensive, so complete" (p. 6)—a revolution the schools cannot ignore. Second, within the crisis there yet is promise of "compensations," for

it is useless to bemoan the departure of the good old days of children's modesty, reverence, and implicit obedience, if we expect merely by bemoaning and by exhortation to bring them back. It is radical conditions which have changed, and only an equally radical change in education suffices. We must recognize our compensations—the increase in toleration, in breadth of social judgment, the larger acquaintance with human nature, the sharpened alertness in reading signs of character and interpreting social situations, greater accuracy of adaptation to differing personalities, contact with greater commercial activities (pp. 8–9).

The third theme is the poverty of the traditional, exclusively "subject-matter," "teacher-disciplinarian" educational system brought to these shores largely uncorrected from Europe. The fourth theme is related to this one, and it is almost Jeffersonian and Whitmanesque:

What the best and wisest parent wants for his own child, that must the community want for all of its children. Any other ideal for our schools is narrow and unlovely; acted upon, it destroys our democracy. . . . Only by being true to the full growth of all the individuals who make it up, can society by any chance be true to itself (p. 5).

It is this last theme that is pursued in several of the chapters, as Dewey tries to find ways whereby the school can be reconstructed to seize new possibilities for revision of curriculum activities and subjects, meshing the possibilities with the newer (then) conceptions of the child's nature as being inherently "dynamic, purposive or growth-oriented," and pluri-potential rather than "fixed" by genetic endowment in any highly unequivocal way.

This latter is a fifth theme: human nature, *each* child's nature, is constantly and spontaneously shaping and being shaped by the changing environment—biological, gross physical, social-cultural, and individual. Hence, an antecedently *fixed* curriculum is always likely to answer only to a bygone time and be partially and significantly irrelevant.

(One cannot forbear remarking how some of Dewey's opponents and detractors, not to mention his uncritical followers, were to seize upon his device of revising the approach to subject matter as not a revision but a rejection of subject matter. Some went so far as to say he rejected learning from books as not a proper way to learn from experience —whereas, it is clear that his attempt was actually to show how one should and can *best* learn from books, how books can function *best* in and *as* experience. (See, e.g., pp. 78ff.)

The same themes are pursued at greater length and in more sophisticated detail in Dewey's grand educational opus, *Democracy and Education*,[2] as well as in what might be called the epilogue of that opus, *Experience and Education*.[3] Other themes appear to qualify and enrich those mentioned here, but probably nowhere in Dewey's other books is there the same freshness, and clarity of writing, on matters educational as here.

Did Dewey solve the problems that have become so much ours? Obviously not. What he did was help formulate them in a way that still makes sense for many of those who demand that their world be organized for understanding— if yet control eludes them. Probably Dewey's importance lies partly in this very fact, that few other ways of looking at the problems have seemed so constantly germane and consistent with the hopes for a genuine democracy in America. This volume, emerging in part as it did from his experience in an educational laboratory, was not thought by Dewey to have clear answers for American education; but it continues to generate hopes and even hypotheses which modern-age educators and lay persons can and do find peculiarly compelling in attempting to cope with the complex American experience.

Urbana, Illinois   Joe R. Burnett
November 1979

2. New York: Macmillan Co., 1916.
3. New York: Macmillan Co., 1938.

The School and Society

Publisher's Note*

The first three chapters of this book were delivered as lectures before an audience of parents and others interested in the University Elementary School, in the month of April of the year 1899. Mr. Dewey revised them in part from a stenographic report, and unimportant changes and the slight adaptations necessary for the press have been made in his absence. The lectures retain therefore the unstudied character as well as the power of the spoken word. As they imply more or less familiarity with the work of the Elementary School, Mr. Dewey's supplementary statement of this has been added.

* To 1899 printing.

Author's Note*

A second printing affords a grateful opportunity for recalling that this little book is a sign of the cooperating thoughts and sympathies of many persons. Its indebtedness to Mrs. Emmons Blaine is partly indicated in the dedication. From my friends Mr. and Mrs. George Herbert Mead came that interest, unflagging attention to detail, and artistic taste which, in my absence, remade colloquial remarks until they were fit to print, and then saw the results through the press with the present attractive result—a mode of authorship made easy, which I recommend to others fortunate enough to possess such friends.

It would be an extended paragraph which should list all the friends whose timely and persisting generosity has made possible the school which inspired and defined the ideas of

* February 1900 printing.

these pages. These friends, I am sure, would be the first to recognize the peculiar appropriateness of especial mention of the names of Mrs. Charles R. Crane and Mrs. William R. Linn.

And the school itself in its educational work is a joint undertaking. Many have engaged in shaping it. The clear and experienced intelligence of my wife is wrought everywhere into its texture. The wisdom, tact, and devotion of its instructors have brought about a transformation of its original amorphous plans into articulate form and substance with life and movement of their own. Whatever the issue of the ideas presented in this book, the satisfaction coming from the cooperation of the diverse thoughts and deeds of many persons in undertaking to enlarge the life of the child will abide.

January 5, 1900.

Author's Note to Second Edition

The present edition includes some slight verbal revisions of the three lectures constituting the first portion of the book. The latter portion is included for the first time, containing material borrowed, with some changes, from the author's contributions to the *Elementary School Record*, long out of print.

The writer may perhaps be permitted a word to express his satisfaction that the educational point of view presented in this book is not so novel as it was fifteen years ago; and his desire to believe that the educational experiment of which the book is an outgrowth has not been without influence in the change.

July, 1915.

1. THE SCHOOL AND SOCIAL PROGRESS

We are apt to look at the school from an individualistic standpoint, as something between teacher and pupil, or between teacher and parent. That which interests us most is naturally the progress made by the individual child of our acquaintance, his normal physical development, his advance in ability to read, write, and figure, his growth in the knowledge of geography and history, improvement in manners, habits of promptness, order, and industry—it is from such standards as these that we judge the work of the school. And rightly so. Yet the range of the outlook needs to be enlarged. What the best and wisest parent wants for his own child, that must the community want for all of its children. Any other ideal for our schools is narrow and unlovely; acted upon, it destroys our democracy. All that society has accomplished for itself is put, through the agency of the school, at the disposal of its future members. All its better thoughts of itself it hopes to realize through the new possibilities thus opened to its future self. Here individualism and socialism are at one. Only by being true to the full growth of all the individuals who make it up, can society by any chance be true to itself. And in the self-direction thus given, nothing counts as much as the school, for, as Horace Mann said, "Where any thing is growing, one former is worth a thousand re-formers."

Whenever we have in mind the discussion of a new movement in education, it is especially necessary to take the broader, or social, view. Otherwise, changes in the school institution and tradition will be looked at as the arbitrary inventions of particular teachers; at the worst transitory fads, and at the best merely improvements in certain details—and this is the plane upon which it is too customary to consider school changes. It is as rational to conceive of the locomotive or the telegraph as personal devices. The modification going

on in the method and curriculum of education is as much a
product of the changed social situation, and as much an effort to meet the needs of the new society that is forming, as
are changes in modes of industry and commerce.

It is to this, then, that I especially ask your attention:
the effort to conceive what roughly may be termed the "New
Education" in the light of larger changes in society. Can we
connect this "New Education" with the general march of
events? If we can, it will lose its isolated character; it will
cease to be an affair which proceeds only from the over-
ingenious minds of pedagogues dealing with particular
pupils. It will appear as part and parcel of the whole social
evolution, and, in its more general features at least, as inevitable. Let us then ask after the main aspects of the social
movement; and afterwards turn to the school to find what
witness it gives of effort to put itself in line. And since it is
quite impossible to cover the whole ground, I shall for the
most part confine myself to one typical thing in the modern
school movement—that which passes under the name of
manual training—hoping if the relation of that to changed
social conditions appears, we shall be ready to concede the
point as well regarding other educational innovations.

I make no apology for not dwelling at length upon the
social changes in question. Those I shall mention are writ so
large that he who runs may read. The change that comes first
to mind, the one that overshadows and even controls all
others, is the industrial one—the application of science resulting in the great inventions that have utilized the forces of
nature on a vast and inexpensive scale: the growth of a
world-wide market as the object of production, of vast manufacturing centres to supply this market, of cheap and rapid
means of communication and distribution between all its
parts. Even as to its feebler beginnings, this change is not
much more than a century old; in many of its most important
aspects it falls within the short span of those now living. One
can hardly believe there has been a revolution in all history
so rapid, so extensive, so complete. Through it the face of the
earth is making over, even as to its physical forms; political
boundaries are wiped out and moved about, as if they were
indeed only lines on a paper map; population is hurriedly

gathered into cities from the ends of the earth; habits of living are altered with startling abruptness and thoroughness; the search for the truths of nature is infinitely stimulated and facilitated, and their application to life made not only practicable, but commercially necessary. Even our moral and religious ideas and interests, the most conservative because the deepest-lying things in our nature, are profoundly affected. That this revolution should not affect education in some other than a formal and superficial fashion is inconceivable.

Back of the factory system lies the household and neighborhood system. Those of us who are here today need go back only one, two, or at most three generations, to find a time when the household was practically the centre in which were carried on, or about which were clustered, all the typical forms of industrial occupation. The clothing worn was for the most part made in the house; the members of the household were usually familiar also with the shearing of the sheep, the carding and spinning of the wool, and the plying of the loom. Instead of pressing a button and flooding the house with electric light, the whole process of getting illumination was followed in its toilsome length, from the killing of the animal and the trying of fat to the making of wicks and dipping of candles. The supply of flour, of lumber, of foods, of building materials, of household furniture, even of metal ware, of nails, hinges, hammers, etc., was produced in the immediate neighborhood, in shops which were constantly open to inspection and often centres of neighborhood congregation. The entire industrial process stood revealed, from the production on the farm of the raw materials till the finished article was actually put to use. Not only this, but practically every member of the household had his own share in the work. The children, as they gained in strength and capacity, were gradually initiated into the mysteries of the several processes. It was a matter of immediate and personal concern, even to the point of actual participation.

We cannot overlook the factors of discipline and of character-building involved in this kind of life: training in habits of order and of industry, and in the idea of responsibility, of obligation to do something, to produce something,

in the world. There was always something which really
needed to be done, and a real necessity that each member of
the household should do his own part faithfully and in cooperation with others. Personalities which became effective
in action were bred and tested in the medium of action.
Again, we cannot overlook the importance for educational
purposes of the close and intimate acquaintance got with
nature at first hand, with real things and materials, with the
actual processes of their manipulation, and the knowledge of
their social necessities and uses. In all this there was continual training of observation, of ingenuity, constructive
imagination, of logical thought, and of the sense of reality
acquired through first-hand contact with actualities. The educative forces of the domestic spinning and weaving, of the
saw-mill, the grist-mill, the cooper shop, and the blacksmith
forge, were continuously operative.

No number of object-lessons, got up *as* object-lessons
for the sake of giving information, can afford even the
shadow of a substitute for acquaintance with the plants and
animals of the farm and garden acquired through actual
living among them and caring for them. No training of sense-
organs in school, introduced for the sake of training, can begin to compete with the alertness and fullness of sense-life
that comes through daily intimacy and interest in familiar
occupations. Verbal memory can be trained in committing
tasks, a certain discipline of the reasoning powers can be
acquired through lessons in science and mathematics; but,
after all, this is somewhat remote and shadowy compared
with the training of attention and of judgment that is acquired in having to do things with a real motive behind and
a real outcome ahead. At present, concentration of industry
and division of labor have practically eliminated household
and neighborhood occupations—at least for educational purposes. But it is useless to bemoan the departure of the good
old days of children's modesty, reverence, and implicit
obedience, if we expect merely by bemoaning and by exhortation to bring them back. It is radical conditions which
have changed, and only an equally radical change in education suffices. We must recognize our compensations—the increase in toleration, in breadth of social judgment, the larger

acquaintance with human nature, the sharpened alertness in reading signs of character and interpreting social situations, greater accuracy of adaptation to differing personalities, contact with greater commercial activities. These considerations mean much to the city-bred child of today. Yet there is a real problem: how shall we retain these advantages, and yet introduce into the school something representing the other side of life—occupations which exact personal responsibilities and which train the child in relation to the physical realities of life?

When we turn to the school, we find that one of the most striking tendencies at present is toward the introduction of so-called manual training, shop-work, and the household arts—sewing and cooking.

This has not been done "on purpose," with a full consciousness that the school must now supply that factor of training formerly taken care of in the home, but rather by instinct, by experimenting and finding that such work takes a vital hold of pupils and gives them something which was not to be got in any other way. Consciousness of its real import is still so weak that the work is often done in a half-hearted, confused, and unrelated way. The reasons assigned to justify it are painfully inadequate or sometimes even positively wrong.

If we were to cross-examine even those who are most favorably disposed to the introduction of this work into our school system, we should, I imagine, generally find the main reasons to be that such work engages the full spontaneous interest and attention of the children. It keeps them alert and active, instead of passive and receptive; it makes them more useful, more capable, and hence more inclined to be helpful at home; it prepares them to some extent for the practical duties of later life—the girls to be more efficient house managers, if not actually cooks and seamstresses; the boys (were our educational system only adequately rounded out into trade schools) for their future vocations. I do not underestimate the worth of these reasons. Of those indicated by the changed attitude of the children I shall indeed have something to say in my next talk, when speaking directly of the relationship of the school to the child. But the point of view is, upon the whole, unnecessarily narrow. We must conceive of work in wood and metal, of weaving, sewing, and cooking, as methods of living and learning, not as distinct studies.

We must conceive of them in their social significance, as types of the processes by which society keeps itself going, as agencies for bringing home to the child some of the primal necessities of community life, and as ways in which these needs have been met by the growing insight and ingenuity of man; in short, as instrumentalities through which the school itself shall be made a genuine form of active community life, instead of a place set apart in which to learn lessons.

A society is a number of people held together because they are working along common lines, in a common spirit, and with reference to common aims. The common needs and aims demand a growing interchange of thought and growing unity of sympathetic feeling. The radical reason that the present school cannot organize itself as a natural social unit is because just this element of common and productive activity is absent. Upon the playground, in game and sport, social organization takes place spontaneously and inevitably. There is something to do, some activity to be carried on, requiring natural divisions of labor, selection of leaders and followers, mutual cooperation and emulation. In the schoolroom the motive and the cement of social organization are alike wanting. Upon the ethical side, the tragic weakness of the present school is that it endeavors to prepare future members of the social order in a medium in which the conditions of the social spirit are eminently wanting.

The difference that appears when occupations are made the articulating centres of school life is not easy to describe in words; it is a difference in motive, of spirit and atmosphere. As one enters a busy kitchen in which a group of children are actively engaged in the preparation of food, the psychological difference, the change from more or less passive and inert recipiency and restraint to one of buoyant outgoing energy, is so obvious as fairly to strike one in the face. Indeed, to those whose image of the school is rigidly set the change is sure to give a shock. But the change in the social attitude is equally marked. The mere absorbing of facts and truths is so exclusively individual an affair that it tends very

naturally to pass into selfishness. There is no obvious social
motive for the acquirement of mere learning, there is no clear
social gain in success thereat. Indeed, almost the only
measure for success is a competitive one, in the bad sense of
that term—a comparison of results in the recitation or in the
examination to see which child has succeeded in getting
ahead of others in storing up, in accumulating, the maximum
of information. So thoroughly is this the prevailing atmosphere that for one child to help another in his task has
become a school crime. Where the school work consists in
simply learning lessons, mutual assistance, instead of being
the most natural form of cooperation and association, becomes a clandestine effort to relieve one's neighbor of his
proper duties. Where active work is going on, all this is
changed. Helping others, instead of being a form of charity
which impoverishes the recipient, is simply an aid in setting
free the powers and furthering the impulse of the one helped.
A spirit of free communication, of interchange of ideas, suggestions, results, both successes and failures of previous experiences, becomes the dominating note of the recitation. So
far as emulation enters in, it is in the comparison of individuals, not with regard to the quantity of information
personally absorbed, but with reference to the quality of
work done—the genuine community standard of value. In an
informal but all the more pervasive way, the school life
organizes itself on a social basis.

Within this organization is found the principle of school
discipline or order. Of course, order is simply a thing which
is relative to an end. If you have the end in view of forty or
fifty children learning certain set lessons, to be recited to a
teacher, your discipline must be devoted to securing that
result. But if the end in view is the development of a spirit of
social cooperation and community life, discipline must grow
out of and be relative to such an aim. There is little of one
sort of order where things are in process of construction;
there is a certain disorder in any busy workshop; there is not
silence; persons are not engaged in maintaining certain fixed
physical postures; their arms are not folded; they are not
holding their books thus and so. They are doing a variety of
things, and there is the confusion, the bustle, that results

from activity. But out of the occupation, out of doing things that are to produce results, and out of doing these in a social and cooperative way, there is born a discipline of its own kind and type. Our whole conception of school discipline changes when we get this point of view. In critical moments we all realize that the only discipline that stands by us, the only training that becomes intuition, is that got through life itself. That we learn from experience, and from books or the sayings of others *only* as they are related to experience, are not mere phrases. But the school has been so set apart, so isolated from the ordinary conditions and motives of life, that the place where children are sent for discipline is the one place in the world where it is most difficult to get experience — the mother of all discipline worth the name. It is only when a narrow and fixed image of traditional school discipline dominates that one is in any danger of overlooking that deeper and infinitely wider discipline that comes from having a part to do in constructive work, in contributing to a result which, social in spirit, is none the less obvious and tangible in form — and hence in a form with reference to which responsibility may be exacted and accurate judgment passed.

The great thing to keep in mind, then, regarding the introduction into the school of various forms of active occupation, is that through them the entire spirit of the school is renewed. It has a chance to affiliate itself with life, to become the child's habitat, where he learns through directed living, instead of being only a place to learn lessons having an abstract and remote reference to some possible living to be done in the future. It gets a chance to be a miniature community, an embryonic society. This is the fundamental fact, and from this arise continuous and orderly streams of instruction. Under the industrial *régime* described, the child, after all, shared in the work, not for the sake of the sharing, but for the sake of the product. The educational results secured were real, yet incidental and dependent. But in the school the typical occupations followed are freed from all economic stress. The aim is not the economic value of the products, but the development of social power and insight. It is this liberation from narrow utilities, this openness to the possibilities of the human spirit that makes these practical activities in the school allies of art and centres of science and history.

The unity of all the sciences is found in geography. The significance of geography is that it presents the earth as the enduring home of the occupations of man. The world without its relationship to human activity is less than a world. Human industry and achievement, apart from their roots in the earth, are not even a sentiment, hardly a name. The earth is the final source of all man's food. It is his continual shelter and protection, the raw material of all his activities, and the home to whose humanizing and idealizing all his achievement returns. It is the great field, the great mine, the great source of the energies of heat, light, and electricity; the great scene of ocean, stream, mountain, and plain, of which all our agriculture and mining and lumbering, all our manufacturing and distributing agencies, are but the partial elements and factors. It is through occupations determined by this environment that mankind has made its historical and political progress. It is through these occupations that the intellectual and emotional interpretation of nature has been developed. It is through what we do in and with the world that we read its meaning and measure its value.

In educational terms, this means that these occupations in the school shall not be mere practical devices or modes of routine employment, the gaining of better technical skill as cooks, seamstresses, or carpenters, but active centres of scientific insight into natural materials and processes, points of departure whence children shall be led out into a realization of the historic development of man. The actual significance of this can be told better through one illustration taken from actual school work than by general discourse.

There is nothing which strikes more oddly upon the average intelligent visitor than to see boys as well as girls of ten, twelve, and thirteen years of age engaged in sewing and weaving. If we look at this from the standpoint of preparation of the boys for sewing on buttons and making patches, we get a narrow and utilitarian conception—a basis that hardly justifies giving prominence to this sort of work in the school. But if we look at it from another side, we find that this work gives the point of departure from which the child can trace and follow the progress of mankind in history, getting an insight also into the materials used and the mechanical principles involved. In connection with these occupations, the historic development of man is recapitulated. For example, the children are first given the raw material — the flax, the cotton plant, the wool as it comes from the back of the sheep (if we could take them to the place where the sheep are sheared, so much the better). Then a study is made of these materials from the standpoint of their adaptation to the uses to which they may be put. For instance, a comparison of the cotton fibre with wool fibre is made. I did not know until the children told me, that the reason for the late development of the cotton industry as compared with the woolen is that the cotton fibre is so very difficult to free by hand from the seeds. The children in one group worked thirty minutes freeing cotton fibres from the boll and seeds, and succeeded in getting out less than one ounce. They could easily believe that one person could gin only one pound a day by hand, and could understand why their ancestors wore woolen instead of cotton clothing. Among other things discovered as affecting their relative utilities was the shortness of the cotton fibre as compared with that of wool, the former averaging, say, one-third of an inch in length, while the latter run to three inches in length; also that the fibres of cotton are smooth and do not cling together, while the wool has a certain roughness which makes the fibres stick, thus assisting the spinning. The children worked this out for themselves with the actual material, aided by questions and suggestions from the teacher.

They then followed the processes necessary for working the fibres up into cloth. They re-invented the first frame for carding the wool — a couple of boards with sharp pins in them for scratching it out. They re-devised the simplest process for spinning the wool — a pierced stone or some other weight through which the wool is passed, and which as it is twirled draws out the fibre; next the top, which was spun on the floor, while the children kept the wool in their hands until it was gradually drawn out and wound upon it. Then the children are introduced to the invention next in historic order, working it out experimentally, thus seeing its necessity, and tracing its effects, not only upon that particular industry, but upon modes of social life—in this way passing in review the entire process up to the present complete loom, and all that goes with the application of science in the use of our present available powers. I need not speak of the science involved in this—the study of the fibres, of geographical features, the conditions under which raw materials are grown, the great centres of manufacture and distribution, the physics involved in the machinery of production; nor, again, of the historical side—the influence which these inventions have had upon humanity. You can concentrate the history of all mankind into the evolution of the flax, cotton, and wool fibres into clothing. I do not mean that this is the only, or the best, centre. But it is true that certain very real and important avenues to the consideration of the history of the race are thus opened—that the mind is introduced to much more fundamental and controlling influences than appear in the political and chronological records that usually pass for history.

Now, what is true of this one instance of fibres used in fabrics (and, of course, I have only spoken of one or two elementary phases of that) is true in its measure of every material used in every occupation, and of the processes employed. The occupation supplies the child with a genuine motive; it gives him experience at first hand; it brings him into contact with realities. It does all this, but in addition it is liberalized throughout by translation into its historic and social values and scientific equivalencies. With the growth of the child's mind in power and knowledge it ceases to be a pleasant occupation merely, and becomes more and more a medium, an instrument, an organ of understanding—and is thereby transformed.

This, in turn, has its bearing upon the teaching of science. Under present conditions, all activity, to be successful, has to be directed somewhere and somehow by the scientific expert—it is a case of applied science. This connection should determine its place in education. It is not only that the occupations, the so-called manual or industrial work in the school, give the opportunity for the introduction of science which illuminates them, which makes them material, freighted with meaning, instead of being mere devices of hand and eye; but that the scientific insight thus gained becomes an indispensable instrument of free and active participation in modern social life. Plato somewhere speaks of the slave as one who in his actions does not express his own ideas, but those of some other man. It is our social problem now, even more urgent than in the time of Plato, that method, purpose, understanding, shall exist in the consciousness of the one who does the work, that his activity shall have meaning to himself.

When occupations in the school are conceived in this broad and generous way, I can only stand lost in wonder at the objections so often heard, that such occupations are out of place in the school because they are materialistic, utilitarian, or even menial in their tendency. It sometimes seems to me that those who make these objections must live in quite another world. The world in which most of us live is a world in which everyone has a calling and occupation, something to do. Some are managers and others are subordinates. But the great thing for one as for the other is that each shall have had the education which enables him to see within his daily work all there is in it of large and human significance. How many of the employed are today mere appendages to the machines which they operate! This may be due in part to the machine itself, or the *régime* which lays so much stress upon the products of the machine; but it is certainly due in large part to the fact that the worker has had no opportunity to develop his imagination and his sympathetic insight as to the social and scientific values found in his work. At present, the impulses which lie at the basis of the industrial system are either practically neglected or positively distorted during the school period. Until the instincts of construction and production are systematically laid hold of in the years of childhood and youth, until they are trained in social directions, enriched by historical interpretation, controlled and illuminated by scientific methods, we certainly are in no position even to locate the source of our economic evils, much less to deal with them effectively.

If we go back a few centuries, we find a practical monopoly of learning. The term *possession* of learning is, indeed, a happy one. Learning was a class matter. This was a necessary result of social conditions. There were not in existence any means by which the multitude could possibly have access to intellectual resources. These were stored up and hidden away in manuscripts. Of these there were at best only a few, and it required long and toilsome preparation to be able to do anything with them. A high-priesthood of learning, which guarded the treasury of truth and which doled it out to the masses under severe restrictions, was the inevitable expression of these conditions. But, as a direct result of the industrial revolution of which we have been speaking, this has been changed. Printing was invented; it was made commercial. Books, magazines, papers were multiplied and cheapened. As a result of the locomotive and telegraph, frequent, rapid, and cheap intercommunication by mails and electricity was called into being. Travel has been rendered easy; freedom of movement, with its accompanying exchange of ideas, indefinitely facilitated. The result has been an intellectual revolution. Learning has been put into circulation. While there still is, and probably always will be, a particular class having the special business of inquiry in hand, a distinctively learned class is henceforth out of the question. It is an anachronism. Knowledge is no longer an immobile solid; it has been liquefied. It is actively moving in all the currents of society itself.

It is easy to see that this revolution, as regards the materials of knowledge, carries with it a marked change in the attitude of the individual. Stimuli of an intellectual sort pour in upon us in all kinds of ways. The merely intellectual life, the life of scholarship and of learning, thus gets a very altered value. Academic and scholastic, instead of being titles of honor, are becoming terms of reproach.

But all this means a necessary change in the attitude of the school, one of which we are as yet far from realizing the full force. Our school methods, and to a very considerable extent our curriculum, are inherited from the period when learning and command of certain symbols, affording as they did the only access to learning, were all-important. The ideals of this period are still largely in control, even where the outward methods and studies have been changed. We

learning, as soon as they have enough of the symbols of reading, writing, and calculating to be of practical use to them in getting a living. While our educational leaders are talking of culture, the development of personality, etc., as the end and aim of education, the great majority of those who pass under the tuition of the school regard it only as a narrowly practical tool with which to get bread and butter enough to eke out a restricted life. If we were to conceive our educational end and aim in a less exclusive way, if we were to introduce into educational processes the activities which appeal to those whose dominant interest is to do and to make, we should find the hold of the school upon its members to be more vital, more prolonged, containing more of culture.

But why should I make this labored presentation? The obvious fact is that our social life has undergone a thorough and radical change. If our education is to have any meaning for life, it must pass through an equally complete transformation. This transformation is not something to appear suddenly, to be executed in a day by conscious purpose. It is already in progress. Those modifications of our school system which often appear (even to those most actively concerned with them, to say nothing of their spectators) to be mere changes of detail, mere improvement within the school mechanism, are in reality signs and evidences of evolution. The introduction of active occupations, of nature study, of elementary science, of art, of history; the relegation of the merely symbolic and formal to a secondary position; the change in the moral school atmosphere, in the relation of pupils and teachers—of discipline; the introduction of more active, expressive, and self-directing factors—all these are not mere accidents, they are necessities of the larger social evolution. It remains but to organize all these factors, to appreciate them in their fullness of meaning, and to put the ideas and ideals involved into complete, uncompromising possession of our school system. To do this means to make each one of our schools an embryonic community life, active with types of occupations that reflect the life of the larger society, and permeated throughout with the spirit of art, history, and science. When the school introduces and trains each child of society into membership within such a little community,

saturating him with the spirit of service, and providing him
with the instruments of effective self-direction, we shall have
the deepest and best guarantee of a larger society which is
worthy, lovely, and harmonious.

2. THE SCHOOL AND THE LIFE OF THE CHILD

Last week I tried to put before you the relationship between the school and the larger life of the community, and the necessity for certain changes in the methods and materials of school work, that it might be better adapted to present social needs.

Today I wish to look at the matter from the other side, and consider the relationship of the school to the life and development of the children in the school. As it is difficult to connect general principles with such thoroughly concrete things as little children, I have taken the liberty of introducing a great deal of illustrative matter from the work of the University Elementary School, that in some measure you may appreciate the way in which the ideas presented work themselves out in actual practice.

Some few years ago I was looking about the school supply stores in the city, trying to find desks and chairs which seemed thoroughly suitable from all points of view—artistic, hygienic, and educational—to the needs of the children. We had a great deal of difficulty in finding what we needed, and finally one dealer, more intelligent than the rest, made this remark: "I am afraid we have not what you want. You want something at which the children may work; these are all for listening." That tells the story of the traditional education. Just as the biologist can take a bone or two and reconstruct the whole animal, so, if we put before the mind's eye the ordinary schoolroom, with its rows of ugly desks placed in geometrical order, crowded together so that there shall be as little moving room as possible, desks almost all of the same size, with just space enough to hold books, pencils and paper, and add a table, some chairs, the bare walls, and possibly a few pictures, we can reconstruct the only educational activity that can possibly go on in such a place. It is all made "for listening"—because simply studying lessons out of a book is only another kind of listening; it marks the dependency of one mind upon another. The attitude of listening means, comparatively speaking, passivity, absorption; that there are certain ready-made materials which are there, which have been prepared by the school superintendent, the board, the teacher, and of which the child is to take in as much as possible in the least possible time.

There is very little place in the traditional schoolroom for the child to work. The workshop, the laboratory, the materials, the tools with which the child may construct, create, and actively inquire, and even the requisite space, have been for the most part lacking. The things that have to do with these processes have not even a definitely recognized place in education. They are what the educational authorities who write editorials in the daily papers generally term "fads" and "frills." A lady told me yesterday that she had been visiting different schools trying to find one where activity on the part of the children preceded the giving of information on the part of the teacher, or where the children had some motive for demanding the information. She visited, she said, twenty-four different schools before she found her first instance. I may add that that was not in this city.

Another thing that is suggested by these schoolrooms, with their set desks, is that everything is arranged for handling as large numbers of children as possible, for dealing with children *en masse*, as an aggregate of units; involving, again, that they be treated passively. The moment children act they individualize themselves; they cease to be a mass, and become the intensely distinctive beings that we are acquainted with out of school, in the home, the family, on the playground, and in the neighborhood.

On the same basis is explicable the uniformity of method and curriculum. If everything is on a "listening" basis, you can have uniformity of material and method. The ear, and the book which reflects the ear, constitute the medium which is alike for all. There is next to no opportunity for adjustment to varying capacities and demands. There is a certain amount—a fixed quantity—of ready-made results and accomplishments to be acquired by all children alike in a given time. It is in response to this demand that the curricu-

lum has been developed from the elementary school up
through the college. There is just so much desirable knowledge, and there are just so many needed technical accomplishments in the world. Then comes the mathematical
problem of dividing this by the six, twelve, or sixteen years
of school life. Now give the children every year just the
proportionate fraction of the total, and by the time they have
finished they will have mastered the whole. By covering so
much ground during this hour or day or week or year, everything comes out with perfect evenness at the end—provided
the children have not forgotten what they have previously
learned. The outcome of all this is Matthew Arnold's report
of the statement, proudly made to him by an educational
authority in France, that so many thousands of children were
studying at a given hour, say eleven o'clock, just such a
lesson in geography; and in one of our own western cities
this proud boast used to be repeated to successive visitors by
its superintendent.

I may have exaggerated somewhat in order to make
plain the typical points of the old education: its passivity of
attitude, its mechanical massing of children, its uniformity
of curriculum and method. It may be summed up by stating
that the centre of gravity is outside the child. It is in the
teacher, the text-book, anywhere and everywhere you please
except in the immediate instincts and activities of the child
himself. On that basis there is not much to be said about
the *life* of the child. A good deal might be said about the
studying of the child, but the school is not the place where
the child *lives*. Now the change which is coming into our
education is the shifting of the centre of gravity. It is a
change, a revolution, not unlike that introduced by Coperni-
cus when the astronomical centre shifted from the earth to
the sun. In this case the child becomes the sun about which
the appliances of education revolve; he is the centre about
which they are organized.

If we take an example from an ideal home, where the
parent is intelligent enough to recognize what is best for the
child, and is able to supply what is needed, we find the child
learning through the social converse and constitution of the
family. There are certain points of interest and value to

him in the conversation carried on: statements are made, inquiries arise, topics are discussed, and the child continually learns. He states his experiences, his misconceptions are corrected. Again the child participates in the household occupations, and thereby gets habits of industry, order, and regard for the rights and ideas of others, and the fundamental habit of subordinating his activities to the general interest of the household. Participation in these household tasks becomes an opportunity for gaining knowledge. The ideal home would naturally have a workshop where the child could work out his constructive instincts. It would have a miniature laboratory in which his inquiries could be directed. The life of the child would extend out of doors to the garden, surrounding fields, and forests. He would have his excursions, his walks and talks, in which the larger world out of doors would open to him.

Now, if we organize and generalize all of this, we have the ideal school. There is no mystery about it, no wonderful discovery of pedagogy or educational theory. It is simply a question of doing systematically and in a large, intelligent, and competent way what for various reasons can be done in most households only in a comparatively meagre and haphazard manner. In the first place, the ideal home has to be enlarged. The child must be brought into contact with more grown people and with more children in order that there may be the freest and richest social life. Moreover, the occupations and relationships of the home environment are not specially selected for the growth of the child; the main object is something else, and what the child can get out of them is incidental. Hence the need of a school. In this school the life of the child becomes the all-controlling aim. All the media necessary to further the growth of the child centre there. Learning?—certainly, but living primarily, and learning through and in relation to this living. When we take the life of the child centred and organized in this way, we do not find that he is first of all a listening being; quite the contrary.

The statement so frequently made that education means "drawing out" is excellent, if we mean simply to contrast it with the process of pouring in. But, after all, it is difficult to connect the idea of drawing out with the ordinary doings of the child of three, four, seven, or eight years of age. He is already running over, spilling over, with activities of all kinds. He is not a purely latent being whom the adult has to approach with great caution and skill in order gradually to draw out some hidden germ of activity. The child is already intensely active, and the question of education is the question of taking hold of his activities, of giving them direction. Through direction, through organized use, they tend toward valuable results, instead of scattering or being left to merely impulsive expression.

If we keep this before us, the difficulty I find uppermost in the minds of many people regarding what is termed the new education is not so much solved as dissolved; it disappears. A question often asked is: If you begin with the child's ideas, impulses and interests, all so crude, so random and scattering, so little refined or spiritualized, how is he going to get the necessary discipline, culture, and information? If there were no way open to us except to excite and indulge these impulses of the child, the question might well be asked. We should either have to ignore and repress the activities, or else to humor them. But if we have organization of equipment and of materials, there is another path open to us. We can direct the child's activities, giving them exercise along certain lines, and can thus lead up to the goal which logically stands at the end of the paths followed.

"If wishes were horses, beggars would ride." Since they are not, since really to satisfy an impulse or interest means to work it out, and working it out involves running up against obstacles, becoming acquainted with materials, exercising ingenuity, patience, persistence, alertness, it of necessity involves discipline—ordering of power—and supplies knowledge. Take the example of the little child who wants to make a box. If he stops short with the imagination or wish, he certainly will not get discipline. But when he attempts to realize his impulse, it is a question of making his idea definite, making it into a plan, of taking the right kind of wood, measuring the parts needed, giving them the necessary proportions, etc. There is involved the preparation of materials, the sawing, planing, the sand-papering, making all the edges and corners to fit. Knowledge of tools and processes is inevitable. If the child realizes his instinct and makes the box, there is plenty of opportunity to gain discipline and perseverance, to exercise effort in overcoming obstacles, and to attain as well a great deal of information.

So undoubtedly the little child who thinks he would like to cook has little idea of what it means or costs, or what it requires. It is simply a desire to "mess around," perhaps to imitate the activities of older people. And it is doubtless possible to let ourselves down to that level and simply humor that interest. But here, too, if the impulse is exercised, utilized, it runs up against the actual world of hard conditions, to which it must accommodate itself; and there again come in the factors of discipline and knowledge. One of the children became impatient recently, at having to work things out by a long method of experimentation, and said: "Why do we bother with this? Let's follow a recipe in a cook-book." The teacher asked the children where the recipe came from, and the conversation showed that if they simply followed this they would not understand the reasons for what they were doing. They were then quite willing to go on with the experimental work. To follow that work will, indeed, give an illustration of just the point in question. Their occupation happened that day to be the cooking of eggs, as making a transition from the cooking of vegetables to that of meats. In order to get a basis of comparison they first summarized the constituent food elements in the vegetables and made a preliminary comparison with those found in meat. Thus they found that the woody fibre or cellulose in vegetables corresponded to the connective tissue in meat, giving the element of form and structure. They found that starch and starchy products were characteristic of the vegetables, that mineral salts were found in both alike, and that there was fat in both—a small quantity in vegetable food and a large amount in animal. They were prepared then to take up the study of albumen as the characteristic feature of animal food, corresponding to starch in the vegetables, and were ready to consider the conditions requisite for the proper treatment of albumen—the eggs serving as the material of experiment.

They experimented first by taking water at various tem-

CHILD'S DRAWING OF A CAVE AND TREES

peratures, finding out when it was scalding, simmering, and boiling hot, and ascertained the effect of the various degrees of temperature on the white of the egg. That worked out, they were prepared, not simply to cook eggs, but to understand the principle involved in the cooking of eggs. I do not wish to lose sight of the universal in the particular incident. For the child simply to desire to cook an egg, and accordingly drop it in water for three minutes, and take it out when he is told, is not educative. But for the child to realize his own impulse by recognizing the facts, materials and conditions involved, and then to regulate his impulse through that recognition, is educative. This is the difference, upon which I wish to insist, between exciting or indulging an interest and realizing it through its direction.

Another instinct of the child is the use of pencil and paper. All children like to express themselves through the medium of form and color. If you simply indulge this interest by letting the child go on indefinitely, there is no growth that is more than accidental. But let the child first

CHILD'S DRAWING OF A FOREST

express his impulse, and then through criticism, question, and suggestion bring him to consciousness of what he has done, and what he needs to do, and the result is quite different. Here, for example, is the work of a seven-year-old child. It is not average work, it is the best work done among the little children, but it illustrates the particular principle of which I have been speaking. They had been talking about the primitive conditions of social life when people lived in caves. The child's idea of that found expression in this way: the cave is neatly set up on the hill side in an impossible way. You see the conventional tree of childhood—a vertical line with horizontal branches on each side. If the child had been allowed to go on repeating this sort of thing day by day, he would be indulging his instinct rather than exercising it. But the child was now asked to look closely at trees, to compare those seen with the one drawn, to examine more closely and consciously into the conditions of his work. Then he drew trees from observation.

Finally he drew again from combined observation,

memory, and imagination. He made again a free illustration, expressing his own imaginative thought, but controlled by detailed study of actual trees. The result was a scene representing a bit of forest; so far as it goes, it seems to me to have as much poetic feeling as the work of an adult, while at the same time its trees are, in their proportions, possible ones, not mere symbols.

If we roughly classify the impulses which are available in the school, we may group them under four heads. There is the social instinct of the children as shown in conversation, personal intercourse, and communication. We all know how self-centred the little child is at the age of four or five. If any new subject is brought up, if he says anything at all, it is: "I have seen that"; or, "My papa or mamma told me about that." His horizon is not large; an experience must come immediately home to him, if he is to be sufficiently interested to relate it to others and seek theirs in return. And yet the egoistic and limited interest of little children is in this manner capable of infinite expansion. The language instinct is the simplest form of the social expression of the child. Hence it is a great, perhaps the greatest of all educational resources.

Then there is the instinct of making—the constructive impulse. The child's impulse to do finds expression first in play, in movement, gesture, and make-believe, becomes more definite, and seeks outlet in shaping materials into tangible forms and permanent embodiment. The child has not much instinct for abstract inquiry. The instinct of investigation seems to grow out of the combination of the constructive impulse with the conversational. There is no distinction between experimental science for little children and the work done in the carpenter shop. Such work as they can do in physics or chemistry is not for the purpose of making technical generalizations or even arriving at abstract truths. Children simply like to do things, and watch to see what will happen. But this can be taken advantage of, can be directed into ways where it gives results of value, as well as be allowed to go on at random.

And so the expressive impulse of the children, the art instinct, grows also out of the communicating and construc-

tive instincts. It is their refinement and full manifestation.
Make the construction adequate, make it full, free, and
flexible, give it a social motive, something to tell, and you
have a work of art. Take one illustration of this in connection with the textile work—sewing and weaving. The
children made a primitive loom in the shop; here the constructive instinct was appealed to. Then they wished to do
something with this loom, to make something. It was the
type of the Indian loom, and they were shown blankets
woven by the Indians. Each child made a design kindred in
idea to those of the Navajo blankets, and the one which
seemed best adapted to the work in hand was selected. The
technical resources were limited, but the coloring and form
were worked out by the children. Examination shows that it
took patience, thoroughness, and perseverance to do the
work. It involved not merely discipline and information of
both a historical sort and the elements of technical design,
but also something of the spirit of art in adequately con-
veying an idea.

One more instance of the connection of the art side
with the constructive side: The children had been studying
primitive spinning and carding, when one of them, twelve
years of age, made a picture of one of the older children
spinning. Here is another piece of work which is not quite
average; it is better than the average. It is an illustration of
two hands and the drawing out of the wool to get it ready
for spinning. This was done by a child eleven years of age.
But, upon the whole, with the younger children especially,
the art impulse is connected mainly with the social instinct—
the desire to tell, to represent.

Now, keeping in mind these fourfold interests—the
interest in conversation or communication; in inquiry, or
finding out things; in making things, or construction; and
in artistic expression—we may say they are the natural resources, the uninvested capital, upon the exercise of which
depends the active growth of the child. I wish to give one
or two illustrations, the first from the work of children
seven years of age. It illustrates in a way the dominant
desire of the children to talk, particularly about folks and
of things in relation to folks. If you observe little children,

REED LIBRARY

TITLE: John Dewey on education : selecte
BARCODE: 1070002780675
DUE DATE: 09-27-14

TITLE: Outside in : minorities and the t
BARCODE: 1070003862923
DUE DATE: 09-27-14

TITLE: The school and society
BARCODE: 1070002785242
DUE DATE: 09-27-14

TITLE: John Dewey : rethinking our time
BARCODE: 1070003274417
DUE DATE: 09-27-14

REED LIBRARY

CHILD'S DRAWING OF HANDS SPINNING

you will find they are interested in the world of things
mainly in its connection with people, as a background and
medium of human concerns. Many anthropologists have told
us there are certain identities in the child interests with
those of primitive life. There is a sort of natural recurrence
of the child mind to the typical activities of primitive peoples; witness the hut which the boy likes to build in the
yard, playing hunt, with bows, arrows, spears, and so on.
Again the question comes: What are we to do with this
interest—are we to ignore it, or just excite and draw it out?
Or shall we get hold of it and direct it to something ahead,
something better? Some of the work that has been planned
for our seven-year-old children has the latter end in view—
to utilize this interest so that it shall become a means of
seeing the progress of the human race. The children begin
by imagining present conditions taken away until they
are in contact with nature at first hand. That takes them
back to a hunting people, to a people living in caves or trees
and getting a precarious subsistence by hunting and fishing.
They imagine as far as possible the various natural physical

conditions adapted to that sort of life; say, a hilly, woody slope, near mountains and a river where fish would be abundant. Then they go on in imagination through the hunting to the semi-agricultural stage, and through the nomadic to the settled agricultural stage. The point I wish to make is that there is abundant opportunity thus given for actual study, for inquiry which results in gaining information. So, while the instinct primarily appeals to the social side, the interest of the child in people and their doings is carried on into the larger world of reality. For example, the children had some idea of primitive weapons, of the stone arrow-head, etc. That provided occasion for the testing of materials as regards their friability, their shape, texture, etc., resulting in a lesson in mineralogy, as they examined the different stones to find which was best suited to the purpose. The discussion of the iron age supplied a demand for the construction of a smelting oven made out of clay, and of considerable size. As the children did not get their drafts right at first, the mouth of the furnace not being in proper relation to the vent as to size and position, instruction in the principles of combustion, the nature of drafts and of fuel, was required. Yet the instruction was not given ready-made; it was first needed, and then arrived at experimentally. Then the children took some material, such as copper, and went through a series of experiments, fusing it, working it into objects; and the same experiments were made with lead and other metals. This work has been also a continuous course in geography, since the children have had to imagine and work out the various physical conditions necessary to the different forms of social life implied. What would be the physical conditions appropriate to pastoral life? to the beginning of agriculture? to fishing? What would be the natural method of exchange between these peoples? Having worked out such points in conversation, they have afterward represented them in maps and sand-molding. Thus they have gained ideas of the various forms of the configuration of the earth, and at the same time have seen them in their relation to human activity, so that they are not simply external facts, but are fused and welded with social conceptions regarding the life and progress of humanity.

CHILD'S DRAWING OF A GIRL SPINNING

The result, to my mind, justifies completely the conviction that children, in a year of such work (of five hours a week altogether), get infinitely more acquaintance with facts of science, geography, and anthropology than they get where information is the professed end and object, where they are simply set to learning facts in fixed lessons. As to discipline, they get more training of attention, more power of interpretation, of drawing inferences, of acute observation and continuous reflection, than if they were put to working out arbitrary problems simply for the sake of discipline.

I should like at this point to refer to the recitation. We all know what it has been—a place where the child shows off to the teacher and the other children the amount of in-

formation he has succeeded in assimilating from the text-
book. From this other standpoint, the recitation becomes pre-
eminently a social meeting place; it is to the school what
the spontaneous conversation is at home, excepting that it
is more organized, following definite lines. The recitation
becomes the social clearing-house, where experiences and
ideas are exchanged and subjected to criticism, where misconceptions are corrected, and new lines of thought and
inquiry are set up.

This change of the recitation from an examination of
knowledge already acquired to the free play of the children's
communicative instinct, affects and modifies all the language
work of the school. Under the old *régime* it was unques-
tionably a most serious problem to give the children a full
and free use of language. The reason was obvious. The
natural motive for language was seldom offered. In the
pedagogical text-books language is defined as the medium of
expressing thought. It becomes that, more or less, to adults
with trained minds, but it hardly needs to be said that language is primarily a social thing, a means by which we give
our experiences to others and get theirs again in return.
When it is taken away from its natural purpose, it is no
wonder that it becomes a complex and difficult problem to
teach language. Think of the absurdity of having to teach
language as a thing by itself. If there is anything the child
will do before he goes to school, it is to talk of the things
that interest him. But when there are no vital interests
appealed to in the school, when language is used simply for
the repetition of lessons, it is not surprising that one of the
chief difficulties of school work has come to be instruction in
the mother-tongue. Since the language taught is unnatural,
not growing out of the real desire to communicate vital
impressions and convictions, the freedom of children in its
use gradually disappears, until finally the high-school
teacher has to invent all kinds of devices to assist in getting
any spontaneous and full use of speech. Moreover, when
the language instinct is appealed to in a social way, there
is a continual contact with reality. The result is that the
child always has something in his mind to talk about, he
has something to say; he has a thought to express, and a

thought is not a thought unless it is one's own. On the traditional method, the child must say something that he has merely learned. There is all the difference in the world between having something to say and having to say something. The child who has a variety of materials and facts wants to talk about them, and his language becomes more refined and full, because it is controlled and informed by realities. Reading and writing, as well as the oral use of language, may be taught on this basis. It can be done in a *related* way, as the outgrowth of the child's social desire to recount his experiences and get in return the experiences of others, directed always through contact with the facts and forces which determine the truth communicated.

I shall not have time to speak of the work of the older children, where the original crude instincts of construction and communication have been developed into something like scientifically directed inquiry, but I will give an illustration of the use of language following upon this experimental work. The work was on the basis of a simple experiment of the commonest sort, gradually leading the children out into geological and geographical study. The sentences that I am going to read seem to me poetic as well as "scientific." "A long time ago when the earth was new, when it was lava, there was no water on the earth, and there was steam all round the earth up in the air, as there were many gases in the air. One of them was carbon dioxide. The steam became clouds, because the earth began to cool off, and after a while it began to rain, and the water came down and dissolved the carbon dioxide from the air." There is a good deal more science in that than probably would be apparent at the outset. It represents some three months of work on the part of the child. The children kept daily and weekly records, but this is part of the summing up of the quarter's work. I call this language poetic, because the child has a clear image and has a personal feeling for the realities imaged. I extract sentences from two other records to illustrate further the vivid use of language when there is a vivid experience back of it. "When the earth was cold enough to condense, the water, with the help of carbon dioxide, *pulled* the calcium out of the rocks into a large body of water where the little animals could get it." The other reads as follows: "When the earth cooled, calcium was in the rocks. Then the carbon dioxide and water united and formed a solution, and, as it ran, it *tore* out the calcium and carried it on to the sea, where there were little animals who took it out of solution." The use of such words as "pulled" and "tore" in connection with the process of chemical combination evidences a personal realization which compels its own appropriate expression.

If I had not taken so much time in my other illustrations, I should like to show how, beginning with very simple material things, the children are led on to larger fields of investigation, and to the intellectual discipline that is the accompaniment of such research. I will simply mention the experiment in which the work began. It consisted in making precipitated chalk, used for polishing metals. The children, with simple apparatus—a tumbler, lime water, and a glass tube—precipitated the calcium carbonate out of the water; and from this beginning went on to a study of the processes by which rocks of various sorts, igneous, sedimentary, etc., had been formed on the surface of the earth and the places they occupy; then to points in the geography of the United States, Hawaii, and Puerto Rico; to the effects of these various bodies of rock, in their various configurations, upon the human occupations; so that this geological record finally rounded itself out into the life of man at the present time. The children saw and felt the connection between these geologic processes taking place ages and ages ago, and the physical conditions determining the industrial occupations of today.

Of all the possibilities involved in the subject, "The School and the Life of the Child," I have selected but one, because I have found that that one gives people more difficulty, is more of a stumbling-block, than any other. One may be ready to admit that it would be most desirable for the school to be a place in which the child should really live, and get a life-experience in which he should delight and find meaning for its own sake. But then we hear this inquiry: How, upon this basis, shall the child get the needed information; how shall he undergo the required discipline? Yes, it has come to this, that with many, if not most, people the normal processes of life appear to be incompatible with getting information and discipline. So I have tried to indicate, in a highly general and inadequate way (for only the school itself, in its daily operation, could give a detailed and worthy representation), how the problem works itself out—how it is possible to lay hold upon the rudimentary instincts of human nature, and, by supplying a proper medium, so to control their expression as not only to facilitate and enrich the growth of the individual child, but also to supply the same results, and far more, of technical information and discipline that have been the ideals of education in the past.

But although I have selected this especial way of approach (as a concession to the question almost universally raised), I am not willing to leave the matter in this more or less negative and explanatory condition. Life is the great thing after all; the life of the child at its time and in its measure, no less than the life of the adult. Strange would it be, indeed, if intelligent and serious attention to what the child *now* needs and is capable of in the way of a rich, valuable, and expanded life should somehow conflict with the needs and possibilities of later, adult life. "Let us live with our children" certainly means, first of all, that our children shall live—not that they shall be hampered and stunted by being forced into all kinds of conditions, the most remote consideration of which is relevancy to the present life of the child. If we seek the kingdom of heaven, educationally, all other things shall be added unto us—which, being interpreted, is that if we identify ourselves with the real instincts and needs of childhood, and ask only after its fullest assertion and growth, the discipline and information and culture of adult life shall all come in their due season.

Speaking of culture reminds me that in a way I have been speaking only of the outside of the child's activity—only of the outward expression of his impulses toward saying, making, finding out, and creating. The real child, it hardly need be said, lives in the world of imaginative values and ideas which find only imperfect outward embodiment. We hear much nowadays about the cultivation of the child's "imagination." Then we undo much of our own talk and work by a belief that the imagination is some special part of

the child that finds its satisfaction in some one particular
direction—generally speaking, that of the unreal and make-
believe, of the myth and made-up story. Why are we so hard
of heart and so slow to believe? The imagination is the
medium in which the child lives. To him there is everywhere
and in everything that occupies his mind and activity at all
a surplusage of value and significance. The question of the
relation of the school to the child's life is at bottom simply
this: Shall we ignore this native setting and tendency, dealing not with the living child at all, but with the dead image
we have erected, or shall we give it play and satisfaction? If
we once believe in life and in the life of the child, then will
all the occupations and uses spoken of, then will all history
and science, become instruments of appeal and materials of
culture to his imagination, and through that to the richness
and the orderliness of his life. Where we now see only the
outward doing and the outward product, there, behind all
visible results, is the re-adjustment of mental attitude, the
enlarged and sympathetic vision, the sense of growing
power, and the willing ability to identify both insight and
capacity with the interests of the world and man. Unless
culture be a superficial polish, a veneering of mahogany
over common wood, it surely is this—the growth of the
imagination in flexibility, in scope, and in sympathy, till the
life which the individual lives is informed with the life of
nature and of society. When nature and society can live in
the schoolroom, when the forms and tools of learning are
subordinated to the substance of experience, then shall
there be an opportunity for this identification, and culture
shall be the democratic password.

3. WASTE IN EDUCATION

The subject announced for today was "Waste in Education." I should like first to state briefly its relation to the two preceding lectures. The first dealt with the school in its social aspects, and the necessary re-adjustments that have to be made to render it effective in present social conditions. The second dealt with the school in relation to the growth of individual children. Now the third deals with the school as itself an institution, in relation both to society and to its own members — the children. It deals with the question of organization, because all waste is the result of the lack of it, the motive lying behind organization being promotion of economy and efficiency. This question is not one of the waste of money or the waste of things. These matters count; but the primary waste is that of human life, the life of the children while they are at school, and afterward because of inadequate and perverted preparation.

So, when we speak of organization, we are not to think simply of the externals; of that which goes by the name "school system" — the school board, the superintendent, and the building, the engaging and promotion of teachers, etc. These things enter in, but the fundamental organization is that of the school itself as a community of individuals, in its relations to other forms of social life. All waste is due to isolation. Organization is nothing but getting things into connection with one another, so that they work easily, flexibly, and fully. Therefore in speaking of this question of waste in education, I desire to call your attention to the isolation of the various parts of the school system, to the lack of unity in the aims of education, to the lack of coherence in its studies and methods.

I have made a chart (I) which, while I speak of the isolations of the school system itself, may perhaps appeal to the eye and save a little time in verbal explanations. A paradoxical friend of mine says there is nothing so obscure as an illustration, and it is quite possible that my attempt to illustrate my point will simply prove the truth of his statement.

The blocks represent the various elements in the school system, and are intended to indicate roughly the length of time given to each division, and also the overlapping, both in time and in subjects studied, of the individual parts of the system. With each block is given the historical conditions in which it arose and its ruling ideal.

The school system, upon the whole, has grown from the top down. During the Middle Ages it was essentially a cluster of professional schools—especially law and theology. Our present university comes down to us from the Middle Ages. I will not say that at present it is a mediæval institution, but it had its roots in the Middle Ages, and it has not outlived all mediæval traditions regarding learning.

The kindergarten, rising with the present century, was a union of the nursery and of the philosophy of Schelling; a wedding of the plays and games which the mother carried on with her children, to Schelling's highly romantic and symbolic philosophy. The elements that came from the actual study of child life—the continuation of the nursery—have remained a life-bringing force in all education; the Schellingesque factors made an obstruction between it and the rest of the school system, brought about isolations.

The line drawn over the top indicates that there is a certain interaction between the kindergarten and the primary school; for, so far as the primary school remained in spirit foreign to the natural interests of child life, it was isolated from the kindergarten, so that it is a problem, at present, to introduce kindergarten methods into the primary school; the problem of the so-called connecting class. The difficulty is that the two are not one from the start. To get a connection the teacher has had to climb over the wall instead of entering in at the gate.

On the side of aims, the ideal of the kindergarten was the moral development of the children, rather than instruction or discipline; an ideal sometimes emphasized to the point of sentimentality. The primary school grew practically

Chart I

Kindergarten
16th Century Moral

Primary—
16th Century Utility

Connecting Class
19th Century

High School or Academy
Renaissance Culture–Discipline

Grammar or Intermediate School
Renaissance Culture–Discipline

Professional Schools
The 19th Century Utility
Mediaeval Culture

University–Graduate
College Schools
Mediaeval Culture–Discipline

Normal
19th Century Utility Culture

Technical Schools
19th Century Utility

out of the popular movement of the sixteenth century, when along with the invention of printing and the growth of commerce, it became a business necessity to know how to read, write, and figure. The aim was distinctly a practical one; it was utility; getting command of these tools, the symbols of learning, not for the sake of learning, but because they gave access to careers in life otherwise closed.

The division next to the primary school is the grammar school. The term is not much used in the West, but is common in the eastern states. It goes back to the time of the revival of learning—a little earlier perhaps than the conditions out of which the primary school originated, and, even when contemporaneous, having a different ideal. It had to do with the study of language in the higher sense; because, at the time of the Renaissance, Latin and Greek connected people with the culture of the past, with the Roman and Greek world. The classic languages were the only means of escape from the limitations of the Middle Ages. Thus there sprang up the prototype of the grammar school, more liberal than the university (so largely professional in character), for the purpose of putting into the hands of the people the key to the old learning, that men might see a world with a larger horizon. The object was primarily culture, secondarily discipline. It represented much more than the present grammar school. It was the liberal element in the college, which, extending downward, grew into the academy and the high school. Thus the secondary school is still in part just a lower college (having an even higher curriculum than the college of a few centuries ago) or a preparatory department to a college, and in part a rounding up of the utilities of the elementary school.

There appear then two products of the nineteenth century, the technical and normal schools. The schools of technology, engineering, etc., are, of course, mainly the development of nineteenth-century business conditions, as the primary school was the development of business conditions of the sixteenth century. The normal school arose because of the necessity for training teachers, with the idea partly of professional drill, and partly that of culture.

Without going more into detail, we have some eight

different parts of the school system as represented on the chart, all of which arose historically at different times, having different ideals in view, and consequently different methods. I do not wish to suggest that all of the isolation, all of the separation, that has existed in the past between the different parts of the school system still persists. One must, however, recognize that they have never yet been welded into one complete whole. The great problem in education on the administrative side is how to unite these different parts.

Consider the training schools for teachers—the normal schools. These occupy at present a somewhat anomalous position, intermediate between the high school and the college, requiring the high-school preparation, and covering a certain amount of college work. They are isolated from the higher subject-matter of scholarship, since, upon the whole, their object has been to train persons *how* to teach, rather than *what* to teach; while, if we go to the college, we find the other half of this isolation—learning *what* to teach, with almost a contempt for methods of teaching. The college is shut off from contact with children and youth. Its members, to a great extent, away from home and forgetting their own childhood, become eventually teachers with a large amount of subject-matter at command, and little knowledge of how this is related to the minds of those to whom it is to be taught. In this division between what to teach and how to teach, each side suffers from the separation.

It is interesting to follow out the interrelation between primary, grammar, and high schools. The elementary school has crowded up and taken many subjects previously studied in the old New England grammar school. The high school has pushed its subjects down. Latin and algebra have been put in the upper grades, so that the seventh and eighth grades are, after all, about all that is left of the old grammar school. They are a sort of amorphous composite, being partly a place where children go on learning what they already have learned (to read, write, and figure), and partly a place of preparation for the high school. The name in some parts of New England for these upper grades was "Intermediate School." The term was a happy one; the work was simply intermediate between something that had been and something that was going to be, having no special meaning on its own account.

Just as the parts are separated, so do the ideals differ —moral development, practical utility, general culture, discipline, and professional training. These aims are each especially represented in some distinct part of the system of education; and with the growing interaction of the parts, each is supposed to afford a certain amount of culture, discipline, and utility. But the lack of fundamental unity is witnessed in the fact that one study is still considered good for discipline, and another for culture; some parts of arithmetic, for example, for discipline and others for use; literature for culture; grammar for discipline; geography partly for utility, partly for culture; and so on. The unity of education is dissipated, and the studies become centrifugal; so much of this study to secure this end, so much of that to secure another, until the whole becomes a sheer compromise and patchwork between contending aims and disparate studies. The great problem in education on the administrative side is to secure the unity of the whole, in the place of a sequence of more or less unrelated and overlapping parts and thus to reduce the waste arising from friction, reduplication and transitions that are not properly bridged.

In this second symbolic diagram (II) I wish to suggest that really the only way to unite the parts of the system is to unite each to life. We can get only an artificial unity so long as we confine our gaze to the school system itself. We must look at it as part of the larger whole of social life. This block (A) in the centre represents the school system as a whole. (1) At one side we have the home, and the two arrows represent the free interplay of influences, materials, and ideas between the home life and that of the school. (2) Below we have the relation to the natural environment, the great field of geography in the widest sense. The school building has about it a natural environment. It ought to be in a garden, and the children from the garden would be led on to surrounding fields, and then into the wider country, with all its facts and forces. (3) Above is represented business life, and the necessity for free play between the school

Chart II

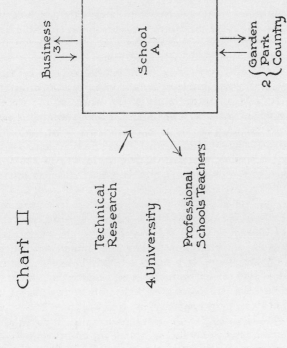

Business
3

1. Home

School
A

2 { Garden
Park
Country

Technical
Research
4. University

Professional
Schools Teachers

and the needs and forces of industry. (4) On the other side
is the university proper, with its various phases, its laboratories, its resources in the way of libraries, museums, and
professional schools.

From the standpoint of the child, the great waste in the
school comes from his inability to utilize the experiences he
gets outside the school in any complete and free way within
the school itself; while, on the other hand, he is unable to
apply in daily life what he is learning at school. That is the
isolation of the school—its isolation from life. When the
child gets into the schoolroom he has to put out of his mind
a large part of the ideas, interests, and activities that pre-
dominate in his home and neighborhood. So the school,
being unable to utilize this everyday experience, sets painfully to work, on another tack and by a variety of means, to
arouse in the child an interest in school studies. While I was
visiting in the city of Moline a few years ago, the superintendent told me that they found many children every year
who were surprised to learn that the Mississippi River in the
text-book had anything to do with the stream of water flow-
ing past their homes. The geography being simply a matter
of the schoolroom, it is more or less of an awakening to many
children to find that the whole thing is nothing but a more
formal and definite statement of the facts which they see,
feel, and touch every day. When we think that we all live on
the earth, that we live in an atmosphere, that our lives are
touched at every point by the influences of the soil, flora, and
fauna, by considerations of light and heat, and then think
of what the school study of geography has been, we have a
typical idea of the gap existing between the everyday experiences of the child, and the isolated material supplied in
such large measure in the school. This is but an instance,
and one upon which most of us may reflect long before we
take the present artificiality of the school as other than a
matter of course or necessity.

Though there should be organic connection between the
school and business life, it is not meant that the school is to
prepare the child for any particular business, but that there
should be a natural connection of the everyday life of the
child with the business environment about him, and that it is

the affair of the school to clarify and liberalize this connection, to bring it to consciousness, not by introducing special studies, like commercial geography and arithmetic, but by keeping alive the ordinary bonds of relation. The subject of compound-business-partnership is probably not in many of the arithmetics nowadays, though it was there not a generation ago, for the makers of text-books said that if they left out anything they could not sell their books. This compound-business-partnership originated as far back as the sixteenth century. The joint-stock company had not been invented, and as large commerce with the Indies and Americas grew up, it was necessary to have an accumulation of capital with which to handle it. One man said, "I will put in this amount of money for six months," and another, "So much for two years," and so on. Thus by joining together they got money enough to float their commercial enterprises. Naturally, then, "compound partnership" was taught in the schools. The joint-stock company was invented; compound partnership disappeared, but the problems relating to it stayed in the arithmetics for two hundred years. They were kept after they had ceased to have practical utility, for the sake of mental discipline—they were "such hard problems, you know." A great deal of what is now in the arithmetics under the head of percentage is of the same nature. Children of twelve and thirteen years of age go through gain and loss calculations, and various forms of bank discount so complicated that the bankers long ago dispensed with them. And when it is pointed out that business is not done this way, we hear again of "mental discipline." And yet there are plenty of real connections between the experience of children and business conditions which need to be utilized and illuminated. The child should study his commercial arithmetic and geography, not as isolated things by themselves, but in their reference to his social environment. The youth needs to become acquainted with the bank as a factor in modern life, with what it does, and how it does it; and then relevant arithmetical processes would have some meaning— quite in contradistinction to the time-absorbing and mind-killing examples in percentage, partial payments, etc., found in all our arithmetics.

The connection with the university, as indicated in this chart, I need not dwell upon. I simply wish to indicate that there ought to be a free interaction between all the parts of the school system. There is much of utter triviality of subject-matter in elementary and secondary education. When we investigate it, we find that it is full of facts taught that are not facts, which have to be unlearned later on. Now, this happens because the "lower" parts of our system are not in vital connection with the "higher." The university or college, in its idea, is a place of research, where investigation is going on, a place of libraries and museums, where the best resources of the past are gathered, maintained and organized. It is, however, as true in the school as in the university that the spirit of inquiry can be got only through and with the attitude of inquiry. The pupil must learn what has meaning, what enlarges his horizon, instead of mere trivialities. He must become acquainted with truths, instead of things that were regarded as such fifty years ago, or that are taken as interesting by the misunderstanding of a partially educated teacher. It is difficult to see how these ends can be reached except as the most advanced part of the educational system is in complete interaction with the most rudimentary.

The next chart (III) is an enlargement of the second. The school building has swelled out, so to speak, the surrounding environment remaining the same, the home, the garden and country, the relation to business life and the university. The object is to show what the school must become to get out of its isolation and secure the organic connection with social life of which we have been speaking. It is not our architect's plan for the school building that we hope to have; but it is a diagrammatic representation of the idea which we want embodied in the school building. On the lower side you see the dining room and the kitchen, at the top the wood and metal shops, and the textile room for sewing and weaving. The centre represents the manner in which all come together in the library, that is to say, in a collection of the intellectual resources of all kinds that throw light upon the practical work, that give it meaning and liberal value. If the four corners represent practice, the interior represents the theory of the practical activities. In other words, the object of

Chart III

Business

Technical Schools
Laboratory
Research

Shop

Textile
Industries

Library
B

Home

University
Library
Museum

Dining
Room

Kitchen

Garden
Park
Country

these forms of practice in the school is not found chiefly in themselves, or in the technical skill of cooks, seamstresses, carpenters and masons, but in their connection, on the social side, with the life without; while on the individual side they respond to the child's need of action, of expression, of desire to do something, to be constructive and creative, instead of simply passive and conforming. Their great significance is that they keep the balance between the social and individual sides—the chart symbolizing particularly the connection with the social. Here on one side is the home. How naturally the lines of connection play back and forth between the home and the kitchen and the textile room of the school! The child can carry over what he learns in the home and utilize it in the school; and the things learned in the school he applies at home. These are the two great things in breaking down isolation, in getting connection—to have the child come to school with all the experience he has got outside the school, and to leave it with something to be immediately used in his everyday life. The child comes to the traditional school with a healthy body and a more or less unwilling mind, though, in fact, he does not bring both his body and mind with him;

he has to leave his mind behind, because there is no way to use it in the school. If he had a purely abstract mind, he could bring it to school with him, but his is a concrete one, interested in concrete things, and unless these things get over into school life, he cannot take his mind with him. What we want is to have the child come to school with a whole mind and a whole body, and leave school with a fuller mind and an even healthier body. And speaking of the body suggests that, while there is no gymnasium in these diagrams, the active life carried on in its four corners brings with it constant physical exercise, while our gymnasium proper will deal with the particular weaknesses of children and their correction, and will attempt more consciously to build up the thoroughly sound body as the abode of the sound mind.

That the dining room and kitchen connect with the country and its processes and products it is hardly necessary to say. Cooking may be so taught that it has no connection with country life, and with the sciences that find their unity in geography. Perhaps it generally has been taught without these connections being really made. But all the materials that come into the kitchen have their origin in the country; they come from the soil, are nurtured through the influences of light and water, and represent a great variety of local environments. Through this connection, extending from the garden into the larger world, the child has his most natural introduction to the study of the sciences. Where did these things grow? What was necessary to their growth? What their relation to the soil? What the effect of different climatic conditions? and so on. We all know what the old-fashioned botany was: partly collecting flowers that were pretty, pressing and mounting them; partly pulling these flowers to pieces and giving technical names to the different parts, finding all the different leaves, naming all their different shapes and forms. It was a study of plants without any reference to the soil, to the country, or to growth. In contrast, a real study of plants takes them in their natural environment and in their uses as well, not simply as food, but in all their adaptations to the social life of man. Cooking becomes as well a most natural introduction to the study of chemistry, giving the child here also something which he can at once bring to bear upon his daily experience. I once heard a very intelligent woman say that she could not understand how science could be taught to little children, because she did not see how they could understand atoms and molecules. In other words, since she did not see how highly abstract facts could be presented to the child independently of daily experience, she could not understand how science could be taught at all. Before we smile at this remark, we need to ask ourselves if she is alone in her assumption, or whether it simply formulates the principle of almost all our school practice.

The same relations with the outside world are found in the carpentry and the textile shops. They connect with the country, as the source of their materials, with physics, as the science of applying energy, with commerce and distribution, with art in the development of architecture and decoration. They have also an intimate connection with the university on the side of its technological and engineering schools; with the laboratory, and its scientific methods and results.

To go back to the square which is marked the library (Chart III, B): if you imagine rooms half in the four corners and half in the library, you will get the idea of the recitation room. That is the place where the children bring the experiences, the problems, the questions, the particular facts which they have found, and discuss them so that new light may be thrown upon them, particularly new light from the experience of others, the accumulated wisdom of the world—symbolized in the library. Here is the organic relation of theory and practice; the child not simply doing things, but getting also the *idea* of what he does; getting from the start some intellectual conception that enters into his practice and enriches it; while every idea finds, directly or indirectly, some application in experience, and has some effect upon life. This, I need hardly say, fixes the position of the "book" or reading in education. Harmful as a substitute for experience, it is all-important in interpreting and expanding experience.

The other chart (IV) illustrates precisely the same idea. It gives the symbolic upper story of this ideal school. In the upper corners are the laboratories; in the lower corners are the studios for art work, both the graphic and auditory arts.

Chart IV

Laboratories
Research

University

Library
Museum

Physical
and Chemical
Laboratories

Biological
Laboratory

Museum

Art

Music

The questions, the chemical and physical problems, arising in the kitchen and shop, are taken to the laboratories to be worked out. For instance, this past week one of the older groups of children doing practical work in weaving which involved the use of the spinning wheel, worked out the diagrams of the direction of forces concerned in treadle and wheel, and the ratio of velocities between wheel and spindle. In the same manner, the plants with which the child has to do in cooking, afford the basis for a concrete interest in botany, and may be taken and studied by themselves. In a certain school in Boston science work for months was centred in the growth of the cotton plant, and yet something new was brought in every day. We hope to do similar work with all the types of plants that furnish materials for sewing and weaving. These examples will suggest, I hope, the relation which the laboratories bear to the rest of the school.

The drawing and music, or the graphic and auditory arts, represent the culmination, the idealization, the highest point of refinement of all the work carried on. I think everybody who has not a purely literary view of the subject recognizes that genuine art grows out of the work of the artisan. The art of the Renaissance was great, because it grew out of the manual arts of life. It did not spring up in a separate atmosphere, however ideal, but carried on to their spiritual meaning processes found in homely and everyday forms of life. The school should observe this relationship. The merely artisan side is narrow, but the mere art, taken by itself, and grafted on from without, tends to become forced, empty, sentimental. I do not mean, of course, that all art work must be correlated in detail to the other work of the school, but simply that a spirit of union gives vitality to the art, and depth and richness to the other work. All art involves physical organs—the eye and hand, the ear and voice; and yet it is something more than the mere technical skill required by the organs of expression. It involves an idea, a thought, a spiritual rendering of things; and yet it is other than any number of ideas by themselves. It is a living union of thought and the instrument of expression. This union is symbolized by saying that in the ideal school the art work might be considered to be that of the shops, passed through the alembic of library and museum into action again.

Take the textile room as an illustration of such a synthesis. I am talking about a future school, the one we hope, some time, to have. The basal fact in that room is that it is a workshop, doing actual things in sewing, spinning, and weaving. The children come into immediate connection with the materials, with various fabrics of silk, cotton, linen and wool. Information at once appears in connection with these materials; their origin, history, their adaptation to particular uses, and the machines of various kinds by which the raw materials are utilized. Discipline arises in dealing with the problems involved, both theoretical and practical. Whence does the culture arise? Partly from seeing all these things reflected through the medium of their scientific and historic conditions and associations, whereby the child learns to appreciate them as technical achievements, as thoughts precipitated in action; and partly because of the introduction of the art idea into the room itself. In the ideal school there would be something of this sort: first, a complete industrial museum, giving samples of materials in various stages of manufacture, and the implements, from the simplest to the most complex, used in dealing with them; then a collection of photographs and pictures illustrating the landscapes and the scenes from which the materials come, their native homes, and their places of manufacture. Such a collection would be a vivid and continual lesson in the synthesis of art, science, and industry. There would be, also, samples of the more perfect forms of textile work, as Italian, French, Japanese, and Oriental. There would be objects illustrating motives of design and decoration which have entered into production. Literature would contribute its part in its idealized representation of the world-industries, as the Penelope in the *Odyssey*—a classic in literature because the character is an adequate embodiment of a certain industrial phase of social life. So, from Homer down to the present time, there is a continuous procession of related facts which have been translated into terms of art. Music lends its share, from the Scotch song at the wheel to the spinning song of Marguerite, or of Wagner's Senta. The shop becomes a pictured museum, appealing to the eye. It would have not only materials,— beautiful woods and designs,—but would give a synopsis of the historical evolution of architecture in its drawings and pictures.

Thus I have attempted to indicate how the school may be connected with life so that the experience gained by the child in a familiar, commonplace way is carried over and made use of there, and what the child learns in the school is carried back and applied in everyday life, making the school an organic whole, instead of a composite of isolated parts. The isolation of studies as well as of parts of the school system disappears. Experience has its geographical aspect, its artistic and its literary, its scientific and its historical sides. All studies arise from aspects of the one earth and the one life lived upon it. We do not have a series of stratified earths, one of which is mathematical, another physical, another historical, and so on. We should not be able to live very long in any one taken by itself. We live in a world where all sides are bound together. All studies grow out of relations in the one great common world. When the child lives in varied but concrete and active relationship to this common world, his studies are naturally unified. It will no longer be a problem to correlate studies. The teacher will not have to resort to all sorts of devices to weave a little arithmetic into the history lesson, and the like. Relate the school to life, and all studies are of necessity correlated.

Moreover, if the school is related as a whole to life as a whole, its various aims and ideals—culture, discipline, information, utility—cease to be variants, for one of which we must select one study and for another another. The growth of the child in the direction of social capacity and service, his larger and more vital union with life, becomes the unifying aim; and discipline, culture and information fall into place as phases of this growth.

I wish to say one word more about the relationship of our particular school to the University. The problem is to unify, to organize, education, to bring all its various factors together, through putting it as a whole into organic union with everyday life. That which lies back of the pedagogical school of the University is the necessity of working out something to serve as a model for such unification, extending from work beginning with the four-year-old child up through the graduate work of the University. Already we have much help from the University in scientific work planned, sometimes even in detail, by heads of the departments. The graduate student comes to us with his researches and methods, suggesting ideas and problems. The library and museum are at hand. We want to bring all things educational together; to break down the barriers that divide the education of the little child from the instruction of the maturing youth; to identify the lower and the higher education, so that it shall be demonstrated to the eye that there is no lower and higher, but simply education.

Speaking more especially with reference to the pedagogical side of the work: I suppose the oldest university chair of pedagogy in our country is about twenty years old—that of the University of Michigan, founded in the latter seventies. But there are only one or two that have tried to make a connection between theory and practice. They teach for the most part by theory, by lectures, by reference to books, rather than through the actual work of teaching itself. At Columbia, through the Teachers College, there is an extensive and close connection between the University and the training of teachers. Something has been done in one or two other places along the same line. We want an even more intimate union here, so that the University shall put all its resources at the disposition of the elementary school, contributing to the evolution of valuable subject-matter and right method, while the school in turn will be a laboratory in which the student of education sees theories and ideas demonstrated, tested, criticized, enforced, and the evolution of new truths. We want the school in its relation to the University to be a working model of a unified education.

A word as to the relation of the school to educational interests generally. I heard once that the adoption of a certain method in use in our school was objected to by a teacher on this ground: "You know that it is an experimental school. They do not work under the same conditions that we are subject to." Now, the purpose of performing an experiment is that other people need not experiment; at least need not experiment so much, may have something definite and positive to go by. An experiment demands particularly favorable conditions in order that results may be reached both freely and securely. It has to work unhampered, with all the needed resources at command. Laboratories lie back of all the great business enterprises of today, back of every great factory, every railway and steamship system. Yet the laboratory is not a business enterprise; it does not aim to secure for itself the conditions of business life, nor does the commercial undertaking repeat the laboratory. There is a difference between working out and testing a new truth, or a new method, and applying it on a wide scale, making it available for the mass of men, making it commercial. But the first thing is to discover the truth, to afford all necessary facilities, for this is the most practical thing in the world in the long run. We do not expect to have other schools literally imitate what we do. A working model is not something to be copied; it is to afford a demonstration of the feasibility of the principle, and of the methods which make it feasible. So (to come back to our own point) we want here to work out the problem of the unity, the organization of the school system in itself, and to do this by relating it so intimately to life as to demonstrate the possibility and necessity of such organization for all education.

4. THREE YEARS OF THE UNIVERSITY ELEMENTARY SCHOOL[1]

The school was started the first week in January, three years ago. I shall try this afternoon to give a brief statement of the ideas and problems that were in mind when the experiment was started, and a sketch of the development of the work since that time. We began in a small house in Fifty-seventh Street, with fifteen children. We found ourselves the next year with twenty-five children in Kimbark Avenue, and then moved in January to Rosalie Court, the larger quarters enabling us to take forty children. The next year the numbers increased to sixty, the school remaining at Rosalie Court. This year we have had ninety-five on the roll at one time, and are located at 5412 Ellis Avenue, where we hope to stay till we have a building and grounds of our own.

The children during the first year of the school were between the ages of six and nine. Now their ages range between four and thirteen—the members of the oldest group being in their thirteenth year. This is the first year that we have children under six, and this has been made possible through the liberality of friends in Honolulu, H. I., who are building up there a memorial kindergarten along the same lines.

The expenses of the school during the first year, of two terms only, were between $1,300 and $1,400. The expenses this year will be about $12,000. Of this amount $5,500 will come from tuitions; $5,000 has been given by friends interested in the school, and there remains about $1,500 yet to be raised for the conduct of the school. This is an indication of the increase of expenses. The average expense per pupil is about the same since the start, i.e., $120 per child per school year. Relatively speaking, this year the expenses of the school took something of a jump, through the expense of moving to a new building, and the repairs and changes there

1. Stenographic report of a talk by John Dewey at a meeting of the Parents' Association of the University Elementary School, February, 1899; somewhat revised.

necessary. An increase in the staff of teachers has also enlarged the work as well as the debits of the school. Next year
(1899–1900) we hope to have about 120 children, and apparently the expenses will be about $2,500 more than this.
Of this amount $2,000 will be met by the increase in tuition
from the pupils. The cost of a child to the school, $120 a
year, is precisely the tuition charged by the University for
students and is double the average tuition charged by the
school. But it is not expected that the University tuition will
come anywhere near meeting the expense involved there.
One reason for not increasing the tuition here, even if it
were advisable for other reasons, is that it is well to
emphasize, from an educational point of view, that elementary as well as advanced education requires endowment.
There is every reason why money should be spent freely for
the organization and maintenance of foundation work in
education as well as for the later stages.

The elementary school has had from the outset two
sides: one, the obvious one of instruction of the children who
have been entrusted to it; the other, relationship to the
University, since the school is under the charge, and forms a
part of the pedagogical work of the University.

When the school was started, there were certain ideas in
mind—perhaps it would be better to say questions and problems; certain points which it seemed worth while to test. If
you will permit one personal word, I should like to say that it
is sometimes thought that the school started out with a
number of ready-made principles and ideas which were to
be put into practice at once. It has been popularly assumed
that I am the author of these ready-made ideas and principles which were to go into execution. I take this opportunity
to say that the educational conduct of the school, as well as
its administration, the selection of subject-matter, and the
working out of the course of study, as well as actual instruction of children, have been almost entirely in the hands
of the teachers of the school; and that there has been a
gradual development of the educational principles and
methods involved, not a fixed equipment. The teachers
started with question marks, rather than with fixed rules,
and if any answers have been reached, it is the teachers in

the school who have supplied them. We started upon the whole with four such questions, or problems:

1. What can be done, and how can it be done, to bring the school into closer relation with the home and neighborhood life—instead of having the school a place where the child comes solely to learn certain lessons? What can be done to break down the barriers which have unfortunately come to separate the school life from the rest of the everyday life of the child? This does not mean, as it is sometimes, perhaps, interpreted to mean, that the child should simply take up in the school things already experienced at home and study them, but that, so far as possible, the child shall have the same attitude and point of view in the school as in the home; that he shall find the same interest in going to school, and in there doing things worth doing for their own sake, that he finds in the plays and occupations which busy him in his home and neighborhood life. It means, again, that the motives which keep the child at work and growing at home shall be used in the school, so that he shall not have to acquire another set of principles of actions belonging only to the school—separate from those of the home. It is a question of the unity of the child's experience, of its actuating motives and aims, not of amusing or even interesting the child.

2. What can be done in the way of introducing subject-matter in history and science and art, that shall have a positive value and real significance in the child's own life; that shall represent, even to the youngest children, something worthy of attainment in skill or knowledge; as much so to the little pupil as are the studies of the high-school or college student to him? You know what the traditional curriculum of the first few years is, even though many modifications have been made. Some statistics have been collected showing that 75 or 80 per cent of the first three years of a child in school are spent upon the form—not the substance—of learning, the mastering of the symbols of reading, writing, and arithmetic. There is not much positive nutriment in this. Its purpose is important—is necessary—but it does not represent the same kind of increase in a child's intellectual and moral experience that is represented by positive truth of

history and nature, or by added insight into reality and beauty. One thing, then, we wanted to find out is how much can be given a child that is really worth his while to get, in knowledge of the world about him, of the forces in the world, of historical and social growth, and in capacity to express himself in a variety of artistic forms. From the strictly educational side this has been the chief problem of the school. It is along this line that we hope to make our chief contribution to education in general; we hope, that is, to work out and publish a positive body of subject-matter which may be generally available.

3. How can instruction in these formal, symbolic branches—the mastering of the ability to read, write, and use figures intelligently—be carried on with everyday experience and occupation as their background and in definite relations to other studies of more inherent content, and be carried on in such a way that the child shall feel their necessity through their connection with subjects which appeal to him on their own account? If this can be accomplished, he will have a vital motive for getting the technical capacity. It is not meant, as has been sometimes jocosely stated, that the child learn to bake and sew at school, and to read, write, and figure at home. It is intended that these formal subjects shall not be presented in such large doses at first as to be the exclusive objects of attention, and that the child shall be led by that which he is doing to feel the need for acquiring skill in the use of symbols and the immediate power they give. In any school, if the child realizes the motive for the use and application of number and language he has taken the longest step toward securing the power; and he can realize the motive only as he has some particular—not some general and remote—use for the symbols.

4. Individual attention. This is secured by small groupings—eight or ten in a class—and a large number of teachers supervising systematically the intellectual needs and attainments and physical well-being and growth of the child. To secure this we have now 135 hours of instructors' time per week, that is, the time of nine teachers for three hours per day, or one teacher per group. It requires but a few words to make this statement about attention to individual powers

and needs, and yet the whole of the school's aims and methods, moral, physical, intellectual, are bound up in it.

I think these four points present a fair statement of what we have set out to discover. The school is often called an experimental school, and in one sense that is the proper name. I do not like to use it too much, for fear parents will think we are experimenting upon the children, and that they naturally object to. But it is an experimental school—at least I hope so—with reference to education and educational problems. We have attempted to find out by trying, by doing—not alone by discussion and theorizing—*whether* these problems may be worked out, and *how* they may be worked out.

Next a few words about the means that have been used in the school in order to test these four questions, and to supply their answers, and first as to the place given to hand-work of different kinds in the school. There are three main lines regularly pursued: (*a*) the shop-work with wood and tools, (*b*) cooking work, and (*c*) work with textiles—sewing and weaving. Of course, there is other hand-work in connection with science, as science is largely of an experimental nature. It is a fact that may not have come to your attention that a large part of the best and most advanced scientific work involves a great deal of manual skill, the training of the hand and eye. It is impossible for one to be a first-class worker in science without this training in manipulation, and in handling apparatus and materials. In connection with the history work, especially with the younger children, hand-work is brought in in the way of making implements, weapons, tools, etc. Of course, the art work is another side—drawing, painting, and modelling. Logically, perhaps, the gymnasium work does not come in here, but as a means of developing moral and intellectual control through the medium of the body it certainly does. The children have one-half hour per day of this form of physical exercise. Along this line we have found that hand-work, in large variety and amount, is the most easy and natural method of keeping up the same attitude of the child in and out of the school. The child gets the largest part of his acquisitions through his bodily activities, until he learns to work systematically with the intellect. That is the purpose of this work in the school, to direct these activities, to systematize and organize them, so that they shall not be as haphazard and as wandering as they are outside of school. The problem of making these forms of practical activity work continuously and definitely together, leading from one factor of skill to another, from one intellectual difficulty to another, has been one of the most difficult, and at the same time one in which we have been most successful. The various kinds of work, carpentry, cooking, sewing, and weaving, are selected as involving different kinds of skill, and demanding different types of intellectual attitude on the part of the child, and because they represent some of the most important activities of the everyday outside world: the question of living under shelter, of daily food and clothing, of the home, of personal movement and exchange of goods. He gets also the training of sense-organs, of touch, of sight, and the ability to coordinate eye and hand. He gets healthy exercise; for the child demands a much larger amount of physical activity than the formal program of the ordinary school permits. There is also a continual appeal to memory, to judgment, in adapting ends to means, a training in habits of order, industry, and neatness in the care of the tools and utensils, and in doing things in a systematic, instead of a haphazard, way. Then, again, these practical occupations make a background, especially in the earlier groups, for the later studies. The children get a good deal of chemistry in connection with cooking, of number work and geometrical principles in carpentry, and a good deal of geography in connection with their theoretical work in weaving and sewing. History also comes in with the origin and growth of various inventions, and their effects upon social life and political organization.

Perhaps more attention, upon the whole, has been given to our second point, that of positive subject-matter, than to any one other thing. On the history side the curriculum is now fairly well worked out. The younger children begin with the home and occupations of the home. In the sixth year the intention is that the children should study occupations outside the home, the larger social industries—farming, mining, lumber, etc.—that they may see the complex and various social industries on which life depends, while incidentally they investigate the use of the various materials—woods, metals, and the processes applied—thus getting a beginning of scientific study. The next year is given to the historical development of industry and invention—starting with man as a savage and carrying him through the typical phases of his progress upward, until the iron age is reached and man begins to enter upon a civilized career. The object of the study of primitive life is not to keep the child interested in lower and relatively savage stages, but to show him the steps of progress and development, especially along the line of invention, by which man was led into civilization. There is a certain nearness, after all, in the child to primitive forms of life. They are much more simple than existing institutions. By throwing the emphasis upon the progress of man, and upon the way advance has been made, we hope to avoid the objections that hold against paying too much attention to the crudities and distracting excitements of savage life.

The next two or three years, *i.e.*, the fourth and fifth grades, and perhaps the sixth, will be devoted to American history. It is then that history, properly speaking, begins, as the study of primitive life can hardly be so called.

Then comes Greek history and Roman, in the regular chronological order, each year having its own work planned with reference to what has come before and after.

The science work was more difficult to arrange and systematize, because there was so little to follow—so little that has been already done in an organized way. We are now at work upon a program,[2] and I shall not speak in detail about it. The first two or three years cultivate the children's powers of observation, lead them to sympathetic interest in the habits of plants and animals, and to look at things with reference to their uses. Then the centre of the work becomes geographical—the study of the earth, as the most central thing. From this almost all the work grows out, and to it the work goes back. Another standpoint in the science work is that of the application of natural forces to the service of man through machines. Last year a good deal of work was done in electricity (and will be repeated this year), based on

2. This year's program is published in the *Elementary School Record*.

the telegraph and telephone—taking up the things that can easily be grasped.

In mechanics they have studied locks and clocks with reference to the adaptation of the various parts of the machinery. All this work makes a most excellent basis for more formal physics later on. Cooking gives opportunity for getting a great many ideas of heat and water, and of their effects. The scientific work taken up in the school differs mainly from that of other schools in having the experimental part— physics and chemistry—emphasized, and is not confined simply to nature study—the study of plants and animals. Not that the latter is less valuable, but that we find it possible to introduce the physical aspects from the first.

If I do not spend a large amount of time in speaking of the music and art work, it is not because they are not considered valuable and important—certainly as much so as any other work done in the school, not only in the development of the child's moral and æsthetic nature, but also from a strictly intellectual point of view. I know of no work in the school that better develops the power of attention, the habit of observation and of consecutiveness, of seeing parts in relation to a whole.

I shall now say a few words about the administrative side of the school. At the outset we mixed up the children of different ages and attainments as much as possible, believing there were mental advantages in the give-and-take thus secured, as well as the moral advantages in having the older assume certain responsibilities in the care of the younger. As the school grew, it became necessary to abandon the method, and to group the children with reference to their common capacities. These groupings, however, are based, not on ability to read and write, but upon similarity of mental attitude and interest, and upon general intellectual capacity and mental alertness. There are ways in which we are still trying to carry out the idea of mixing up the children, that we may not build the rigid stepladder system of the "graded" school. One step in this direction is having the children move about and come in contact with different teachers. While there are difficulties and evils connected with this, I think one of the most useful things in the school is that children come into intimate relation with a number of different personalities. The children also meet in general assemblies—for singing, and for the report of the whole school work as read by members of the different groups. The older children are also given a half hour a week in which to join some of the younger groups, and, if possible, as in hand-work, enter into the work of the younger children. In various ways we are attempting to keep a family spirit throughout the school, and not the feeling of isolated classes and grades.

The organization of the teaching force has gradually become departmental, as the needs of the work have indicated its chief branches. So we now have recognized divisions of Science, History, Domestic or Household Arts, Manual Training in the limited sense (wood and metals), Music, Art (that is, drawing, water colors, clay-modelling, etc.), and Gymnasium. As the work goes on into the secondary period, the languages and mathematics will also of necessity assume a more differentiated and distinct position. As it is sometimes said that correlated or thoroughly harmonized work cannot be secured upon this basis, I am happy to say that our experience shows positively that there are no intrinsic difficulties. Through common devotion to the best development of the child, through common loyalty to the main aims and methods of the school, our teachers have demonstrated that in education, as in business, the best organization is secured through proper regard for natural divisions of labor, interest, and training. The child secures the advantage in discipline and knowledge of contact with experts in each line, while the individual teachers serve the common thought in diverse ways, thus multiplying and reinforcing it.

Upon the moral side, that of so-called discipline and order, where the work of the University Elementary School has perhaps suffered most from misunderstanding and misrepresentation, I shall say only that our ideal has been, and continues to be, that of the best form of family life, rather than that of a rigid graded school. In the latter, the large number of children under the care of a single teacher, and the very limited number of modes of activity open to the pupils, have made necessary certain fixed and somewhat external forms of "keeping order." It would be very stupid to copy these, under the changed conditions of our school, its small groups permitting and requiring the most intimate personal acquaintance of child and teacher, and its great variety of forms of work, with their differing adaptations to the needs of different children. If we have permitted to our children more than the usual amount of freedom, it has not been in order to relax or decrease real discipline, but because under our particular conditions larger and less artificial responsibilities could thus be required of the children, and their entire development of body and spirit be more harmonious and complete. And I am confident that the parents who have entrusted their children to us for any length of time will agree in saying that, while the children like, or love, to come to school, yet work, and not amusement, has been the spirit and teaching of the school; and that this freedom has been granted under such conditions of intelligent and sympathetic oversight as to be a means of upbuilding and strengthening character.

At the end of three years, then, we are not afraid to say that some of our original questions have secured affirmative answers. The increase of our children from fifteen to almost one hundred, along with a practical doubling of fees, has shown that parents are ready for a form of education that makes individual growth its sole controlling aim. The presence of an organized corps of instructors demonstrates that thoroughly educated teachers are ready to bring to elementary education the same resources of training, knowledge, and skill that have long been at the command of higher education. The everyday work of the school shows that children can live in school as out of it, and yet grow daily in wisdom, kindness, and the spirit of obedience—that learning may, even with little children, lay hold upon the substance of truth that nourishes the spirit, and yet the forms of knowledge be observed and cultivated; and that growth may be genuine and thorough, and yet a delight.

5. THE PSYCHOLOGY OF ELEMENTARY EDUCATION

Naturally, most of the public is interested in what goes on day by day in a school in direct relation to the children there. This is true of parents who send their boys and girls for the sake of the personal results they wish to secure, not for the sake of contributing to educational theory. In the main, it is true of visitors to a school who recognize, in varying degrees, what is actually done with the children before their eyes, but who rarely have either the interest or the time to consider the work in relation to underlying problems. A school cannot lose sight of this aspect of its work, since only by attending to it can the school retain the confidence of its patrons and the presence of its pupils.

Nevertheless a school conducted by a department of a university must have another aspect. From the university standpoint, the most important part of its work is the scientific—the contribution it makes to the progress of educational thinking. The aim of educating a certain number of children would hardly justify a university in departing from the tradition which limits it to those who have completed their secondary instruction. Only the scientific aim, the conduct of a laboratory, comparable to other scientific laboratories, can furnish a reason for the maintenance by a university of an elementary school. Such a school is a laboratory of applied psychology. That is, it has a place for the study of mind as manifested and developed in the child, and for the search after materials and agencies that seem most likely to fulfill and further the conditions of normal growth.

It is not a normal school or a department for the training of teachers. It is not a model school. It is not intended to demonstrate any one special idea or doctrine. Its task is the problem of viewing the education of the child in the light of the principles of mental activity and processes of growth made known by modern psychology. The problem by its nature is an infinite one. All that any school can do is to make contributions here and there, and to stand for the necessity of considering education, both theoretically and practically, in this light. This being the end, the school conditions must, of course, agree. To endeavor to study the process and laws of growth under such artificial conditions as prevent many of the chief facts of child life from showing themselves is an obvious absurdity.

In its practical aspect, this laboratory problem takes the form of the construction of a course of study which harmonizes with the natural history of the growth of the child in capacity and experience. The question is the selection of the kind, variety, and due proportion of subjects, answering most definitely to the dominant needs and powers of a given period of growth, and of those modes of presentation that will cause the selected material to enter vitally into growth. We cannot admit too fully or too freely the limits of our knowledge and the depths of our ignorance in these matters. No one has a complete hold scientifically upon the chief psychological facts of any one year of child life. It would be sheer presumption to claim that just the material best fitted to promote this growth has as yet been discovered. The assumption of an educational laboratory is rather that enough is known of the conditions and modes of growth to make intelligent inquiry possible; and that it is only by acting upon what is already known that more can be found out. The chief point is such experimentation as will add to our reasonable convictions. The demand is to secure arrangements that will permit and encourage freedom of investigation; that will give some assurance that important facts will not be forced out of sight; conditions that will enable the educational practice indicated by the inquiry to be sincerely acted upon, without the distortion and suppression arising from undue dependence upon tradition and preconceived notions. It is in this sense that the school would be an experimental station in education.

What, then, are the chief working hypotheses that have been adopted from psychology? What educational counterparts have been hit upon as in some degree in line with the adopted psychology?

The discussion of these questions may be approached by

pointing out a contrast between contemporary psychology and the psychology of former days. The contrast is a triple one. Earlier psychology regarded mind as a purely individual affair in direct and naked contact with an external world. The only question asked was of the ways in which the world and the mind acted upon each other. The entire process recognized would have been in theory exactly the same if there were one mind living alone in the universe. At present the tendency is to conceive individual mind as a function of social life — as not capable of operating or developing by itself, but as requiring continual stimulus from social agencies, and finding its nutrition in social supplies. The idea of heredity has made familiar the notion that the equipment of the individual, mental as well as physical, is an inheritance from the race: a capital inherited by the individual from the past and held in trust by him for the future. The idea of evolution has made familiar the notion that mind cannot be regarded as an individual, monopolistic possession, but represents the outworkings of the endeavor and thought of humanity; that it is developed in an environment which is social as well as physical, and that social needs and aims have been most potent in shaping it — and the chief difference between savagery and civilization is not in the naked nature which each faces, but the social heredity and social medium.

Studies of childhood have made it equally apparent that this socially acquired inheritance operates in the individual only under present social stimuli. Nature must indeed furnish its physical stimuli of light, sound, heat, etc., but the significance attaching to these, the interpretation made of them, depends upon the ways in which the society in which the child lives acts and reacts in reference to them. The bare physical stimulus of light is not the entire reality; the interpretation given to it through social activities and thinking confers upon it its wealth of meaning. It is through imitation, suggestion, direct instruction, and even more indirect unconscious tuition, that the child learns to estimate and treat the bare physical stimuli. It is through the social agencies that he recapitulates in a few short years the progress which it has taken the race slow centuries to work out.

Educational practice has exhibited an unconscious

adaptation to and harmony with the prevailing psychology; both grew out of the same soil. Just as mind was supposed to get its filling by direct contact with the world, so all the needs of instruction were thought to be met by bringing the child mind into direct relation with various bodies of external fact labelled geography, arithmetic, grammar, etc. That these classified sets of facts were simply selections from the social life of the past was overlooked; equally so that they had been generated out of social situations and represented the answers found for social needs. No social element was found in the subject-matter nor in the intrinsic appeal which it made to the child; it was located wholly outside in the teacher—in the encouragements, admonitions, urgings, and devices of the instructor in getting the child's mind to work upon a material which in itself was only accidentally lighted up by any social gleam. It was forgotten that the maximum appeal, and the full meaning in the life of the child, could be secured only when the studies were presented not as bare external studies, but from the standpoint of the relation they bear to the life of society. It was forgotten that to become integral parts of the child's conduct and character they must be assimilated not as mere items of information, but as organic parts of his present needs and aims—which in turn are social.

In the second place, the older psychology was a psychology of knowledge, of intellect. Emotion and endeavor occupied but an incidental and derivative place. Much was said about sensations—next to nothing about movements. There was discussion of ideas and of whether they originated in sensations or in some innate mental faculty; but the possibility of their origin in and from the needs of action was ignored. Their influence upon conduct, upon behavior, was regarded as an external attachment. Now we believe (to use the words of Mr. James) that the intellect, the sphere of sensations and ideas, is but a "middle department which we sometimes take to be final, failing to see, amid the monstrous diversity of the length and complication of the cogitations which may fill it, that it can have but one essential function—the function of defining the direction which our activity, immediate or remote, shall take."

Here also was a preëstablished harmony between educational practice and psychological theory. Knowledge in the schools was isolated and made an end in itself. Facts, laws, information have been the staple of the curriculum. The controversy in educational theory and practice was between those who relied more upon the sense-element in knowledge, upon contact with things, upon object-lessons, etc., and those who emphasized abstract ideas, generalizations, etc.—reason, so-called, but in reality other people's ideas as formulated in books. In neither case was there any attempt to connect either the sense-training or the logical operations with the problems and interests of the life of practice. Here again an educational transformation is indicated if we are to suppose that our psychological theories stand for any truths of life.

The third point of contrast lies in the modern conception of the mind as essentially a process—a process of growth, not a fixed thing. According to the older view mind was mind, and that was the whole story. Mind was the same throughout, because fitted out with the same assortment of faculties whether in child or adult. If any difference was made it was simply that some of these ready-made faculties—such as memory—came into play at an earlier time, while others, such as judging and inferring, made their appearance only after the child, through memorizing drills, had been reduced to complete dependence upon the thought of others. The only important difference that was recognized was one of quantity, of amount. The boy was a little man and his mind was a little mind—in everything but the size the same as that of the adult, having its own ready-furnished equipment of faculties of attention, memory, etc. Now we believe in the mind as a growing affair, and hence as essentially changing, presenting distinctive phases of capacity and interest at different periods. These are all one and the same in the sense of continuity of life, but all different in that each has its own distinctive claims and offices. "First the blade, then the ear, and then the full corn in the ear."

It is hardly possible to overstate the agreement of education and psychology at this point. The course of study was thoroughly, even if unconsciously, controlled by the assumption that since mind and its faculties are the same

throughout, the subject-matter of the adult, logically arranged facts and principles, is the natural "study" of the
child—simplified and made easier of course, since the wind
must be tempered to the shorn lamb. The outcome was the
traditional course of study in which again child and adult
minds are absolutely identified, except as regards the mere
matter of amount or quantity of power. The entire range of
the universe is first subdivided into sections called studies;
then each one of these studies is broken up into bits, and
some one bit assigned to a certain year of the course. No
order of development was recognized—it was enough that the
earlier parts were made easier than the later. To use the
pertinent illustration of Mr. W. S. Jackman in stating the
absurdity of this sort of curriculum: "It must seem to
geography teachers that Heaven smiled on them when it
ordained but four or five continents, because starting in far
enough along the course it was so easy, that it really seemed
to be natural, to give one continent to each grade, and then
come out right in the eight years."

If once more we are in earnest with the idea of mind
as growth, this growth carrying with it typical features distinctive of its various stages, it is clear that an educational
transformation is again indicated. It is clear that the selection and grading of material in the course of study must be
done with reference to proper nutrition of the dominant
directions of activity in a given period, not with reference to
chopped-up sections of a ready-made universe of knowledge.

It is, of course, comparatively easy to lay down general
propositions like the foregoing; easy to use them to criticize
existing school conditions; easy by means of them to urge the
necessity of something different. But art is long. The difficulty is in carrying such conceptions into effect—in seeing
just what materials and methods, in what proportion and
arrangement, are available and helpful at a given time. Here
again we must fall back upon the idea of the laboratory.
There is no answer in advance to such questions as these.
Tradition does not give it because tradition is founded upon
a radically different psychology. Mere reasoning cannot give
it because it is a question of fact. It is only by trying that
such things can be found out. To refuse to try, to stick blindly

to tradition, because the search for the truth involves experimentation in the region of the unknown, is to refuse the only step which can introduce rational conviction into education.

Hence the following statement simply reports various lines of inquiry started during the last five years, with some of the results more recently indicated. These results can, of course, make no claim to be other than tentative, excepting in so far as a more definite consciousness of what the problems are, clearing the way for more intelligent action in the future, is a definitive advance. It should also be stated that practically it has not as yet been possible, in many cases, to act adequately upon the best ideas obtained, because of administrative difficulties, due to lack of funds—difficulties centering in the lack of a proper building and appliances, and in inability to pay the amounts necessary to secure the complete time of teachers in some important lines. Indeed, with the growth of the school in numbers, and in the age and maturity of pupils, it is becoming a grave question how long it is fair to the experiment to carry it on without more adequate facilities.

In coming now to speak of the educational answers which have been sought for the psychological hypotheses, it is convenient to start from the matter of the stages of growth. The first stage (found in the child say of from four to eight years of age) is characterized by directness of social and personal interests, and by directness and promptness of relationship between impressions, ideas, and action. The demand for a motor outlet for expression is urgent and immediate. Hence the subject-matter for these years is selected from phases of life entering into the child's own social surroundings, and, as far as may be, capable of reproduction by him in something approaching social form—in play, games, occupations, or miniature industrial arts, stories, pictorial imagination, and conversation. At first the material is such as lies nearest the child himself, the family life and its neighborhood setting; it then goes on to something slightly more remote, social occupations (especially those having to do with the interdependence of city and country life), and then extends itself to the historical evolution of typical occupations and of the social forms connected with them. The

material is not presented as lessons, as something to be learned, but rather as something to be taken up into the child's own experience, through his own activities, in weaving, cooking, shop-work, modelling, dramatic plays, conversation, discussion, story-telling, etc. These in turn are direct agencies. They are forms of motor or expressive activity. They are emphasized so as to dominate the school program, in order that the intimate connection between knowing and doing, so characteristic of this period of child life, may be maintained. The aim, then, is not for the child to go to school as a place apart, but rather in the school so to recapitulate typical phases of his experience outside of school, as to enlarge, enrich, and gradually formulate it.

In the second period, extending from eight or nine to eleven or twelve, the aim is to recognize and respond to the change which comes into the child from his growing sense of the possibility of more permanent and objective results, and of the necessity for the control of agencies for the skill necessary to reach these results. When the child recognizes distinct and enduring ends which stand out and demand attention on their own account, the previous vague and fluid unity of life is broken up. The mere play of activity no longer directly satisfies. It must be felt to accomplish something—to lead up to a definite and abiding outcome. Hence the recognition of rules of action—that is, of regular means appropriate to reaching permanent results—and of the value of mastering special processes so as to give skill in their use.

Hence, on the educational side, the problem is, as regards the subject-matter, to differentiate the vague unity of experience into characteristic typical phases, selecting such as clearly illustrate the importance to mankind of command over specific agencies and methods of thought and action in realizing its highest aims. The problem on the side of method is an analogous one: to bring the child to recognize the necessity of a similar development within himself—the need of securing for himself practical and intellectual control of such methods of work and inquiry as will enable him to realize results for himself.

On the more direct social side, American history (especially that of the period of colonization) is selected as furnishing a typical example of patience, courage, ingenuity,

and continual judgment in adapting means to ends, even in the face of great hazard and obstacle; while the material itself is so definite, vivid, and human as to come directly within the range of the child's representative and constructive imagination and thus becomes, vicariously at least, a part of his own expanding consciousness. Since the aim is not "covering the ground," but knowledge of social processes used to secure social results, no attempt is made to go over the entire history, in chronological order, of America. Rather a series of types is taken up: Chicago and the northwestern Mississippi valley; Virginia, New York, and the Puritans and Pilgrims in New England. The aim is to present a variety of climatic and local conditions, to show the different sorts of obstacles and helps that people found, and a variety of historic traditions, and customs and purposes of different people.

The method involves presentation of a large amount of detail, of minutiæ of surroundings, tools, clothing, household utensils, foods, modes of living day by day, so that the child can reproduce the material as life, not as mere historic information. In this way, social processes and results become realities. Moreover, to the personal and dramatic identification of the child with the social life studied, characteristic of the earlier period, there now supervenes an *intellectual* identification—the child puts himself at the standpoint of the problems that have to be met and rediscovers, so far as may be, ways of meeting them.

The general standpoint—the adaptation of means to ends—controls also the work in science. For purposes of convenience, this may be regarded as now differentiated into two sides—the geographical and the experimental. Since, as just stated, the history work depends upon an appreciation of the natural environment as affording resources and presenting urgent problems, considerable attention is paid to the physiography, mountains, rivers, plains, and lines of natural travel and exchange, flora and fauna of each of the colonies. This is connected with field excursions in order that the child may be able to supply from observation, as far as possible, the data to be used by constructive imagination, in reproducing more remote environments.

The experimental side devotes itself to a study of

processes which yield typical results of value to men. The activity of the child in the earlier period is directly productive, rather than investigative. His experiments are modes of active doing—almost as much so as his play and games. Later he tries to find out how various materials or agencies are manipulated in order to give certain results. It is thus clearly distinguished from experimentation in the scientific sense—such as is appropriate to the secondary period—where the aim is the discovery of facts and verification of principles. Since the practical interest predominates, it is a study of applied science rather than of pure science. For instance, processes are selected found to have been of importance in colonial life—bleaching, dyeing, soap and candle-making, manufacture of pewter dishes, making of cider and vinegar, leading to some study of chemical agencies, of oils, fats, elementary metallurgy. "Physics" is commenced from the same applied standpoint. A study is made of the use and transfer of energy in the spinning-wheel and looms; everyday uses of mechanical principles are taken up—in locks, scales, etc., going on later to electric appliances and devices—bells, the telegraph, etc.

The relation of means to ends is emphasized also in other lines of work. In art, attention is given to practical questions of perspective, of proportion of spaces and masses, balance, effect of color combinations and contrasts, etc. In cooking, the principles of food-composition and of effects of various agencies upon these elements are taken up, so that the children may deduce, as far as possible, their own rules. In sewing, methods of cutting, fitting (as applied to dolls' clothing) come up, and later on the technical sequence of stitches, etc.

It is clear that with the increasing differentiation of lines of work and interest, leading to greater individuality and independence in various studies, great care must be taken to find the balance between, on one side, undue separation and isolation, and on the other, a miscellaneous and casual attention to a large number of topics, without adequate emphasis and distinctiveness to any. The first principle makes work mechanical and formal, divorces it from the life-experience of the child, and from effective in-

fluence upon conduct. The second makes it scrappy and
vague, and leaves the child without definite command of
his own powers, or clear consciousness of purposes. It is
perhaps only in the present year that the specific principle of
the conscious relation of means to ends has emerged as the
unifying principle of this period; and it is hoped that emphasis of this in all lines of work will have a decidedly cumu-
lative and unifying effect upon the child's development.

Nothing has been said, as yet, of one of the most important agencies or means in extending and controlling
experience—command of the social or conventional symbols
—symbols of language, including those of quantity. The
importance of these instrumentalities is so great that the
traditional or three R's curriculum is based upon them—
from 60 to 80 per cent of the time program of the first four
or five years of elementary schools being devoted to them,
the smaller figure representing selected rather than average
schools.

These subjects are social in a double sense. They represent the tools which society has evolved in the past as the
instruments of its intellectual pursuits. They represent the
keys which will unlock to the child the wealth of social
capital which lies beyond the possible range of his limited
individual experience. While these two points of view must
always give these arts a highly important place in education,
they also make it necessary that certain conditions should be
observed in their introduction and use. In a wholesale and
direct application of the studies no account is taken of these
conditions. The chief problem at present relating to the
three R's is recognition of these conditions and the adaptation of work to them.

The conditions may be reduced to two: (1) The need
that the child shall have in his own personal and vital experience a varied background of contact and acquaintance
with realities, social and physical. This is necessary to prevent symbols from becoming a purely second-hand and conventional substitute for reality. (2) The need that the more
ordinary, direct, and personal experience of the child shall
furnish problems, motives, and interests that necessitate recourse to books for their solution, satisfaction, and pursuit.

Otherwise, the child approaches the book without intellectual hunger, without alertness, without a questioning attitude, and the result is the one so deplorably common: such abject dependence upon books as weakens and cripples vigor of thought and inquiry, combined with reading for mere random stimulation of fancy, emotional indulgence, and flight from the world of reality into a make-belief land.

The problem here is then (1) to furnish the child with a sufficiently large amount of personal activity, in occupations, expression, conversation, construction, and experimentation, so that his individuality, moral and intellectual, shall not be swamped by a disproportionate amount of the experience of others to which books introduce him; and (2) so to conduct this more direct experience as to make the child feel the need of resort to and command of the traditional social tools—furnish him with motives and make his recourse to them intelligent, an addition to his powers, instead of a servile dependency. When this problem shall be solved, work in language, literature, and number will not be a combination of mechanical drill, formal analysis and appeal, even if unconscious, to sensational interests; and there will not be the slightest reason to fear that books and all that relates to them will not take the important place to which they are entitled.

It is hardly necessary to say that the problem is not yet solved. The common complaint that children's progress in these traditional school studies is sacrificed to the newer subjects that have come into the curriculum is sufficient evidence that the exact balance is not yet struck. The experience thus far in the school, even if not demonstrative, indicates the following probable results: (1) the more direct modes of activity, constructive and occupation work, scientific observation, experimentation, etc., present plenty of opportunities and occasions for the necessary use of reading, writing (and spelling), and number work. These things may be introduced, then, not as isolated studies, but as organic outgrowths of the child's experience. The problem is, in a systematic and progressive way, to take advantage of these occasions. (2) The additional vitality and meaning which these studies thus secure make possible a very considerable reduction of the time ordinarily devoted to them. (3) The final use of the symbols, whether in reading, calculation, or composition, is more intelligent, less mechanical; more active, less passively receptive; more an increase of power, less a mere mode of enjoyment.

On the other hand, increasing experience seems to make clear the following points: (1) that it is possible, in the early years, to appeal, in teaching the recognition and use of symbols, to the child's power of production and creation; as much so in principle as in other lines of work seemingly much more direct, and that there is the advantage of a limited and definite result by which the child may measure his progress. (2) Failure sufficiently to take account of this fact results in an undue postponement of some phases of these lines of work, with the effect that the child, having progressed to a more advanced plane intellectually, feels what earlier might have been a form of power and creation to be an irksome task. (3) There is a demand for periodic concentration and alternation in the school program of the time devoted to these studies—and of all studies where mastery of technique or special method is advisable. That is to say, instead of carrying all subjects simultaneously and at an equal pace upon the program, at times one must be brought to the foreground and others relegated to the background, until the child is brought to the point of recognizing that he has a power or skill, which he can now go ahead and use independently.

The third period of elementary education is upon the borderland of secondary. It comes when the child has a sufficient acquaintance of a fairly direct sort with various forms of reality and modes of activity; and when he has sufficiently mastered the methods, the tools of thought, inquiry, and activity, appropriate to various phases of experience, to be able profitably to specialize upon distinctive studies and arts for technical and intellectual aims. While the school has a number of children who are in this period, the school has not, of course, been in existence long enough so that any typical inferences can be safely drawn. There certainly seems to be reason to hope, however, that with the consciousness of difficulties, needs, and resources gained in

the experience of the last five years, children can be brought
to and through this period without sacrifice of thoroughness,
mental discipline, or command of technical tools of learning, and with a positive enlargement of life, and a wider,
freer, and more open outlook upon it.

6. FROEBEL'S EDUCATIONAL PRINCIPLES

One of the traditions of the Elementary School of the University of Chicago is of a visitor who, in its early days, called to see the kindergarten. On being told that the school had not as yet established one, she asked if there were not singing, drawing, manual training, plays and dramatizations, and attention to the children's social relations. When her questions were answered in the affirmative, she remarked, both triumphantly and indignantly, that that was what she understood by a kindergarten, and that she did not know what was meant by saying that the school had no kindergarten. The remark was perhaps justified in spirit, if not in letter. At all events, it suggests that in a certain sense the school endeavors throughout its whole course—now including children between four and thirteen—to carry into effect certain principles which Froebel was perhaps the first consciously to set forth. Speaking still in general, these principles are:

1. That the primary business of school is to train children in cooperative and mutually helpful living; to foster in them the consciousness of mutual interdependence; and to help them practically in making the adjustments that will carry this spirit into overt deeds.

2. That the primary root of all educative activity is in the instinctive, impulsive attitudes and activities of the child, and not in the presentation and application of external material, whether through the ideas of others or through the senses; and that, accordingly, numberless spontaneous activities of children, plays, games, mimic efforts, even the apparently meaningless motions of infants—exhibitions previously ignored as trivial, futile, or even condemned as positively evil—are capable of educational use; nay, are the foundation stones of educational method.

3. That these individual tendencies and activities are

organized and directed through the uses made of them in
keeping up the cooperative living already spoken of; taking
advantage of them to reproduce on the child's plane the
typical doings and occupations of the larger, maturer society
into which he is finally to go forth; and that it is through
production and creative use that valuable knowledge is secured and clinched.

So far as these statements correctly represent Froebel's
educational philosophy, the school should be regarded as its
exponent. An attempt is making to act upon them with as
much faith and sincerity in their application to children of
twelve as to children of four. This attempt, however, to
assume what might be called the kindergarten attitude
throughout the whole school makes necessary certain modifications of the work done in what is more technically known
as the kindergarten period—that is, with the children between the ages of four and six. It is necessary only to state
reasons for believing that in spite of the apparently radical
character of some of them they are true to the spirit of
Froebel.

As Regards Play and Games

Play is not to be identified with anything which the
child externally does. It rather designates his mental attitude in its entirety and in its unity. It is the free play, the
interplay, of all the child's powers, thoughts, and physical
movements, in embodying, in a satisfying form, his own
images and interests. Negatively, it is freedom from economic pressure—the necessities of getting a living and sup-
porting others—and from the fixed responsibilities attaching
to the special callings of the adult. Positively, it means that
the supreme end of the child is fullness of growth—fullness
of realization of his budding powers, a realization which
continually carries him on from one plane to another.

This is a very general statement, and taken in its
generality is so vague as to be innocent of practical bearing.
Its significance in detail, in application, however, means the
possibility, and in many respects the necessity, of quite a

radical change of kindergarten procedure. To state it baldly, the fact that "play" denotes the psychological attitude of the child, not his outward performances, means complete emancipation from the necessity of following any given or prescribed system, or sequence of gifts, plays, or occupations. The judicious teacher will certainly look for suggestions to the activities mentioned by Froebel (in his *Mother Play* and elsewhere), and to those set forth in such minute detail by his disciples; but she will also remember that the principle of play requires her carefully to investigate and criticize these things, and decide whether they are really activities for her own children, or just things which may have been vital in the past to children living in different social conditions. So far as occupations, games, etc., simply perpetuate those of Froebel and his earlier disciples, it may fairly be said that in many respects the presumption is against them—the presumption is that in the worship of the external doings discussed by Froebel we have ceased to be loyal to his principle.

The teacher must be absolutely free to get suggestions from any and from every source, asking herself but these two questions: Will the proposed mode of play appeal to the child as his own? Is it something of which he has the instinctive roots in himself, and which will mature the capacities that are struggling for manifestation in him? And again: Will the proposed activity give that sort of expression to these impulses that will carry the child on to a higher plane of consciousness and action, instead of merely exciting him, and then leaving him just where he was before, plus a certain amount of nervous exhaustion and appetite for more excitation in the future?

There is every evidence that Froebel studied carefully— inductively we might now say—the children's plays of his own time, and the games which mothers played with their infants. He also took great pains—as in his *Mother Play*—to point out that certain principles of large import were involved. He had to bring his generation to consciousness of the fact that these things were not merely trivial and childish because done by children, but were essential factors in their growth. But I do not see the slightest evidence that he supposed that just these plays, and only these plays, had meaning, or that his philosophic explanation had any motive beyond that just suggested. On the contrary, I believe that he expected his followers to exhibit their following by continuing his own study of contemporary conditions and activities, rather than by literally adhering to the plays he had collected. Moreover, it is hardly likely that Froebel himself would contend that in his interpretation of these games he did more than take advantage of the best psychological and philosophical insight available to him at the time; and we may suppose that he would have been the first to welcome the growth of a better and more extensive psychology (whether general, experimental, or as child-study), and would avail himself of its results to reinterpret the activities, to discuss them more critically, going from the new standpoint into the reasons that make them educationally valuable.

Symbolism

It must be remembered that much of Froebel's symbolism is the product of two peculiar conditions of his own life and work. In the first place, on account of inadequate knowledge at that time of the physiological and psychological facts and principles of child growth, he was often forced to resort to strained and artificial explanations of the value attaching to the plays, etc. To the impartial observer it is obvious that many of his statements are cumbrous and farfetched, giving abstract philosophical reasons for matters that may now receive a simple, everyday formulation. In the second place, the general political and social conditions of Germany were such that it was impossible to conceive continuity between the free, cooperative social life of the kindergarten and that of the world outside. Accordingly, he could not regard the "occupations" of the schoolroom as literal reproductions of the ethical principles involved in community life—the latter were often too restricted and authoritative to serve as worthy models.

Accordingly he was compelled to think of them as symbolic of abstract ethical and philosophical principles. There certainly is change enough and progress enough in the social conditions of the United States of today, as compared with those of the Germany of his day, to justify making kindergarten activities more natural, more direct, and more real representations of current life than Froebel's disciples have done. Even as it is, the disparity of Froebel's philosophy with German political ideals has made the authorities in Germany suspicious of the kindergarten, and has been undoubtedly one force operating in transforming its social simplicity into an involved intellectual technique.

Imagination and Play

An excessive emphasis on symbolism is sure to influence the treatment of imagination. It is of course true that a little child lives in a world of imagination. In one sense, he can only "make believe." His activities represent or stand for the life that he sees going on around him. Because they are thus representative they may be termed symbolic, but it should be remembered that this make-believe or symbolism has reference to the activities suggested. Unless they are, to the child, as real and definite as the adult's activities are to him, the inevitable result is artificiality, nervous strain, and either physical and emotional excitement, or else deadening of powers.

There has been a curious, almost unaccountable, tendency in the kindergarten to assume that because the value of the activity lies in what it stands for to the child, therefore the materials used must be as artificial as possible, and that one must keep carefully away from real things and real acts on the part of the child. Thus one hears of gardening activities which are carried on by sprinkling grains of sand for seeds; the child sweeps and dusts a make-believe room with make-believe brooms and cloths; he sets a table using only paper cut in the flat (and even then cut with reference to geometric design, rather than to dishes), instead of toy tea things with which the child outside of the kindergarten plays. Dolls, toy locomotives, and trains of cars, etc., are tabooed as altogether too grossly real—and hence not cultivating the child's imagination.

All this is surely mere superstition. The imaginative play of the child's mind comes through the cluster of suggestions, reminiscences, and anticipations that gather about the things he uses. The more natural and straightforward these are, the more definite basis there is for calling up and holding together all the allied suggestions which make his imaginative play really representative. The simple cooking, dish-washing, dusting, etc., which children do are no more prosaic or utilitarian to them than would be, say, the game of the Five Knights. To the children these occupations are surcharged with a sense of the mysterious values that attach to whatever their elders are concerned with. The materials, then, must be as "real," as direct and straightforward, as opportunity permits.

But the principle does not end here—the reality symbolized must also lie within the capacities of the child's own appreciation. It is sometimes thought the use of the imagination is profitable in the degree it stands for very remote metaphysical and spiritual principles. In the great majority of such cases it is safe to say that the adult deceives himself. He is conscious of both the reality and the symbol, and hence of the relation between them. But since the truth or reality represented is far beyond the reach of the child, the supposed symbol is not a symbol to him at all. It is simply a positive thing on its own account. Practically about all he gets out of it is its own physical and sensational meaning, plus, very often, a glib facility in phrases and attitudes that he learns are expected of him by the teacher—without, however, any mental counterpart. We often teach insincerity, and instill sentimentalism, and foster sensationalism when we think we are teaching spiritual truths by means of symbols. The realities reproduced, therefore, by the child should be of as familiar, direct, and real a character as possible. It is largely for this reason that in the kindergarten of our school the work centres so much about the reproduction of home and neighborhood life. This brings us to the topic of

Subject-matter

The home life in its setting of house, furniture, utensils, etc., together with the occupations carried on in the home, offers, accordingly, material which is in a direct and real relationship to the child, and which he naturally tends to reproduce in imaginative form. It is also sufficiently full of ethical relations and suggestive of moral duties to afford plenty of food for the child on his moral side. The program is comparatively unambitious compared with that of many kindergartens, but it may be questioned whether there are not certain positive advantages in this limitation of the subject-matter. When much ground is covered (the work going over, say, industrial society, army, church, state, etc.), there is a tendency for the work to become over-symbolic. So much of this material lies beyond the experience and capacities of the child of four and five that practically all he gets out of it is the physical and emotional reflex—he does not get any real penetration into the material itself. Moreover, there is danger, in these ambitious programs, of an unfavorable reaction upon the child's own intellectual attitude. Having covered pretty much the whole universe in a purely make-believe fashion, he becomes blasé, loses his natural hunger for the simple things of direct experience, and approaches the material of the first grades of the primary school with a feeling that he has had all that already. The later years of a child's life have their own rights, and a superficial, merely emotional anticipation is likely to do the child serious injury.

Moreover, there is danger that a mental habit of jumping rapidly from one topic to another be induced. The little child has a good deal of patience and endurance of a certain type. It is true that he has a liking for novelty and variety; that he soon wearies of an activity that does not lead out into new fields and open up new paths for exploration. My plea, however, is not for monotony. There is sufficient variety in the activities, furnishings, and instrumentalities of the homes from which the children come to give continual diversity. It touches the civic and the industrial life at this and that point; these concerns can be brought in, when desirable, without going beyond the unity of the main topic. Thus there is an opportunity to foster that sense which is at the basis of attention, and of all intellectual growth, a sense of continuity.

This continuity is often interfered with by the very methods that aim at securing it. From the child's standpoint unity lies in the subject-matter—in the present case, in the fact that he is always dealing with one thing: home life. Emphasis is continually passing from one phase of this life to another; one occupation after another, one piece of furniture after another, one relation after another, etc., receive attention; but they all fall into building up one and the same mode of living, although bringing now this feature, now that, into prominence. The child is working all the time *within a unity*, giving different phases of its clearness and definiteness, and bringing them into coherent connection with each other. When there is a great diversity of subject-matter, continuity is apt to be sought simply on the formal side; that is, in schemes of sequence, "schools of work," a rigid program of development followed with every topic, a "thought for the day" from which the work is not supposed to stray. As a rule such sequence is purely intellectual, hence is grasped only by the teacher, quite passing over the head of the child. Hence the program for the year, term, month, week, etc., should be made out on the basis of estimating how much of the common subject-matter can be covered in that time, not on the basis of intellectual or ethical principles. This will give both definiteness and elasticity.

Method

The peculiar problem of the early grades is, of course, to get hold of the child's natural impulses and instincts, and to utilize them so that the child is carried on to a higher plane of perception and judgment, and equipped with more efficient habits; so that he has an enlarged and deepened consciousness, and increased control of powers of action. Wherever this result is not reached, play results in mere amusement and not in educative growth.

Upon the whole, constructive or "built up" work (with, of course, the proper alternation of story, song, and game which may be connected, so far as is desirable, with the ideas involved in the construction) seems better fitted than anything else to secure these two factors—initiation in the child's own impulse and termination upon a higher plane. It brings the child in contact with a great variety of material: wood, tin, leather, yarn, etc.; it supplies a motive for using these materials in real ways instead of going through exercises having no meaning except a remote symbolic one; it calls into play alertness of the senses and acuteness of observation; it demands clear-cut imagery of the ends to be accomplished, and requires ingenuity and invention in planning; it makes necessary concentrated attention and personal responsibility in execution, while the results are in such tangible form that the child may be led to judge his own work and improve his standards.

A word should be said regarding the psychology of imitation and suggestion in relation to kindergarten work. There is no doubt that the little child is highly imitative and open to suggestions; there is no doubt that his crude powers and immature consciousness need to be continually enriched and directed through these channels. But on this account it is imperative to discriminate between a use of imitation and suggestion which is so external as to be thoroughly nonpsychological, and a use which is justified through its organic relation to the child's own activities. As a general principle no activity should be *originated* by imitation. The start must come from the child; the model or copy may then be supplied in order to assist the child in imaging more definitely what it is that he really wants—in bringing him to consciousness. Its value is not as model to copy in action, but as guide to clearness and adequacy of conception. Unless the child can get away from it to his own imagery when it comes to execution, he is rendered servile and dependent, not developed. Imitation comes in to reinforce and help out, not to initiate.

There is no ground for holding that the teacher should not suggest anything to the child until he has *consciously* expressed a want in that direction. A sympathetic teacher is quite likely to know more clearly than the child himself what his own instincts are and mean. But the suggestion must *fit in* with the dominant mode of growth in the child; it must serve simply as stimulus to bring forth more adequately what the child is already blindly striving to do. Only by watching the child and seeing the attitude that he assumes toward suggestions can we tell whether they are operating as factors in furthering the child's growth, or whether they are external, arbitrary impositions interfering with normal growth.

The same principle applies even more strongly to so-called dictation work. Nothing is more absurd than to suppose that there is no middle term between leaving a child to his own unguided fancies and likes or controlling his activities by a formal succession of dictated directions. As just intimated, it is the teacher's business to know what powers are striving for utterance at a given period in the child's development, and what sorts of activity will bring these to helpful expression, in order then to supply the requisite stimuli and needed materials. The suggestion, for instance, of a playhouse, the suggestion that comes from seeing objects that have already been made to furnish it, from seeing other children at work, is quite sufficient definitely to direct the activities of a normal child of five. Imitation and suggestion come in naturally and inevitably, but only as instruments to help him carry out his own wishes and ideas. They serve to make him realize, to bring to consciousness, what he already is striving for in a vague, confused, and therefore ineffective way. From the psychological standpoint it may safely be said that when a teacher has to rely upon a series of dictated directions, it is just because the child has no image of his own of what is to be done or why it is to be done. Instead, therefore, of gaining power of control by conforming to directions, he is really losing it—made dependent upon an external source.

In conclusion, it may be pointed out that such subject-matter and the method connect directly with the work of the six-year-old children (corresponding to the first grade of primary work). The play reproduction of the home life passes naturally on into a more extended and serious study of the larger social occupations upon which the home is dependent; while the continually increasing demands made upon the child's own ability to plan and execute carry him over into more controlled use of attention upon more distinctively intellectual topics. It must not be forgotten that the readjustment needed to secure continuity between "kindergarten" and "first-grade" work cannot be brought about wholly from the side of the latter. The school change must be as gradual and insensible as that in the growth of the child. This is impossible unless the subprimary work surrenders whatever isolates it, and hospitably welcomes whatever materials and resources will keep pace with the full development of the child's powers, and thus keep him always prepared, ready, for the next work he has to do.

7. THE PSYCHOLOGY OF OCCUPATIONS

By occupation is not meant any kind of "busy work" or exercises that may be given to a child in order to keep him out of mischief or idleness when seated at his desk. By occupation I mean a mode of activity on the part of the child which reproduces, or runs parallel to, some form of work carried on in social life. In the University Elementary School these occupations are represented by the shop-work with wood and tools; by cooking, sewing, and by the textile work.

The fundamental point in the psychology of an occupation is that it maintains a balance between the intellectual and the practical phases of experience. As an occupation it is active or motor; it finds expression through the physical organs—the eyes, hands, etc. But it also involves continual observation of materials, and continual planning and reflection, in order that the practical or executive side may be successfully carried on. Occupation as thus conceived must, therefore, be carefully distinguished from work which educates primarily for a trade. It differs because its end is in itself; in the growth that comes from the continual interplay of ideas and their embodiment in action, not in external utility.

It is possible to carry on this type of work in other than trade schools, so that the entire emphasis falls upon the manual or physical side. In such cases the work is reduced to a mere routine or custom, and its educational value is lost. This is the inevitable tendency wherever, in manual training for instance, the mastery of certain tools, or the production of certain objects, is made the primary end, and the child is not given, wherever possible, intellectual responsibility for selecting the materials and instruments that are most fit, and given an opportunity to think out his own model and plan of work, led to perceive his own errors, and find out how to correct them—that is, of course, within the range of his capacities. So far as the external result is held in view, rather than the mental and moral states and growth involved in the process of reaching the result, the work may be called manual, but cannot rightly be termed an occupation. Of course the tendency of all mere habit, routine, or custom is to result in what is unconscious and mechanical. That of occupation is to put the maximum of consciousness into whatever is done.

This enables us to interpret the stress laid (*a*) upon personal experimenting, planning, and re-inventing in connection with the textile work, and (*b*) its parallelism with lines of historical development. The first requires the child to be mentally quick and alert at every point in order that he may do the outward work properly. The second enriches and deepens the work performed by saturating it with values suggested from the social life which it recapitulates.

Occupations, so considered, furnish the ideal occasions for both sense-training and discipline in thought. The weakness of ordinary lessons in observation, calculated to train the senses, is that they have no outlet beyond themselves, and hence no necessary motive. Now, in the natural life of the individual and the race there is always a reason for sense-observation. There is always some need, coming from an end to be reached, that makes one look about to discover and discriminate whatever will assist him. Normal sensations operate as clues, as aids, as stimuli, in directing activity in what has to be done; they are not ends in themselves. Separated from real needs and motives, sense-training becomes a mere gymnastic and easily degenerates into acquiring what are hardly more than mere knacks or tricks in observation, or else mere excitement of the sense-organs.

The same principle applies in normal *thinking*. It also does not occur for its own sake, nor end in itself. It arises from the need of meeting some difficulty, in reflecting upon the best way of overcoming it, and thus leads to planning, to projecting mentally the result to be reached, and deciding upon the steps necessary and their serial order. This concrete logic of action long precedes the logic of pure speculation or abstract investigation, and through the mental habits that it forms is the best of preparations for the latter.

Another educational point upon which the psychology

of occupations throws helpful light is the place of interest in
school work. One of the objections regularly brought against
giving in school work any large or positive place to the
child's interest is the impossibility on such a basis of proper
selection. The child, it is said, has all kinds of interests,
good, bad, and indifferent. It is necessary to decide between
the interests that are really important and those that are
trivial; between those that are helpful and those that are
harmful; between those that are transitory or mark immediate excitement, and those which endure and are permanently
influential. It would seem as if we had to go beyond interest
to get any basis for using interest.

Now, there can be no doubt that occupation-work
possesses a strong interest for the child. A glance into any
school where such work is carried on will give sufficient
evidence of this fact. Outside of the school, a large portion
of the children's plays are simply more or less miniature and
haphazard attempts at reproducing social occupations. There
are certain reasons for believing that the type of interest
which springs up along with these occupations is of a
thoroughly healthy, permanent, and really educative sort;
and that by giving a larger place to occupations we should
secure an excellent, perhaps the very best, way of making
an appeal to the child's spontaneous interest, and yet have,
at the same time, some guarantee that we are not dealing
with what is merely pleasure-giving, exciting, or transient.

In the first place, every interest grows out of some
instinct or some habit that in turn is finally based upon an
original instinct. It does not follow that all instincts are of
equal value, or that we do not inherit many instincts which
need transformation, rather than satisfaction, in order to be
useful in life. But the instincts which find their conscious
outlet and expression in occupation are bound to be of an
exceedingly fundamental and permanent type. The activities
of life are of necessity directed to bringing the materials and
forces of nature under the control of our purposes; of making
them tributary to ends of life. Men have had to work in order
to live. In and through their work they have mastered nature,
they have protected and enriched the conditions of their own
life, they have been awakened to the sense of their own

powers—have been led to invent, to plan, and to rejoice in
the acquisition of skill. In a rough way, all occupations may
be classified as gathering about man's fundamental relations
to the world in which he lives through getting food to maintain life; securing clothing and shelter to protect and orna-
ment it, and thus, finally, to provide a permanent home in
which all the higher and more spiritual interests may centre.
It is hardly unreasonable to suppose that interests which
have such a history behind them must be of the worthy sort.

However, these interests as they develop in the child not
only recapitulate past important activities of the race, but
reproduce those of the child's present environment. He continually sees his elders engaged in such pursuits. He daily
has to do with things which are the results of just such
occupations. He comes in contact with facts that have no
meaning, except in reference to them. Take these things out
of the present social life and see how little would remain—
and this not only on the material side, but as regards intellectual, æsthetic, and moral activities, for these are largely
and necessarily bound up with occupations. The child's instinctive interests in this direction are, therefore, constantly
reinforced by what he sees, feels, and hears going on around
him. Suggestions along this line are continually coming to
him; motives are awakened; his energies are stirred to action.
Again, it is not unreasonable to suppose that interests which
are touched so constantly, and on so many sides, belong to
the worthy and enduring type.

In the third place, one of the objections made against
the principle of interest in education is that it tends to dis-
integration of mental economy by constantly stirring up the
child in this way or that, destroying continuity and thoroughness. But an occupation (such as the textile one) is of necessity a continuous thing. It lasts not only for days, but for
months and years. It represents, not a stirring of isolated
and superficial energies, but rather a steady, continuous organization of power along certain general lines. The same is
true, of course, of any other form of occupation, such as
shop-work with tools, or as cooking. The occupations articulate a vast variety of impulses, otherwise separate and
spasmodic, into a consistent skeleton with a firm backbone.

It may well be doubted whether, wholly apart from some such regular and progressive modes of action, extending as cores throughout the entire school, it would be permanently safe to give the principle of "interest" any large place in school work.

8. THE DEVELOPMENT OF ATTENTION

The subprimary or kindergarten department is undertaking the pedagogical problems growing out of an attempt to connect kindergarten work intimately with primary, and to readapt traditional materials and technique to meet present social conditions and our present physiological and psychological knowledge.

Little children have their observations and thoughts mainly directed towards people: what they do, how they behave, what they are occupied with, and what comes of it. Their interest is of a personal rather than of an objective or intellectual sort. Its intellectual counterpart is the story-form, not the task, consciously defined end, or problem—meaning by story-form something psychical, the holding together of a variety of persons, things, and incidents through a common idea that enlists feeling; not an outward relation or tale. Their minds seek wholes, varied through episode, enlivened with action and defined in salient features—there must be go, movement, the sense of use and operation—inspection of things separated from the idea by which they are carried. Analysis of isolated detail of form and structure neither appeals nor satisfies.

Material provided by existing social occupations is calculated to meet and feed this attitude. In previous years the children have been concerned with the occupations of the home, and the contact of homes with one another and with outside life. Now they may take up typical occupations of society at large—a step farther removed from the child's egoistic, self-absorbed interest, and yet dealing with something personal and something which touches him.

From the standpoint of educational theory, the following features may be noted:

1. The study of natural objects, processes, and relations is placed in a human setting. During the year, a con-

siderably detailed observation of seeds and their growth, of plants, woods, stones, animals, as to some phases of structure and habit, of geographical conditions of landscape, climate, arrangement of land and water, is undertaken. The pedagogical problem is to direct the child's power of observation, to nurture his sympathetic interest in characteristic traits of the world in which he lives, to afford interpreting material for later more special studies, and yet to supply a carrying medium for the variety of facts and ideas through the dominant spontaneous emotions and thoughts of the child. Hence their association with human life. Absolutely no separation is made between the "social" side of the work, its concern with people's activities and their mutual dependencies, and the "science," regard for physical facts and forces—because the conscious distinction between man and nature is the result of later reflection and abstraction, and to force it upon the child here is not only to fail to engage his whole mental energy, but to confuse and distract him. The environment is always that in which life is situated and through which it is circumstanced; and to isolate it, to make it with little children an object of observation and remark by itself, is to treat human nature inconsiderately. At last, the original open and free attitude of the mind to nature is destroyed; nature has been reduced to a mass of meaningless details.

In its emphasis upon the "concrete" and "individual," modern pedagogical theory often loses sight of the fact that the existence and presentation of an individual physical thing—a stone, an orange, a cat—is no guarantee of *concreteness*—that this is a psychological affair, whatever appeals to the mind as a whole, as a self-sufficient centre of interest and attention. The reaction from this external and somewhat dead standpoint often assumes, however, that the needed clothing with human significance can come only by direct personification, and we have that continued symbolization of a plant, cloud or rain which makes only pseudo-science possible; which, instead of generating love for nature itself, switches interest to certain sensational and emotional accompaniments, and leaves it, at last, dissipated and burnt out. And even the tendency to approach nature through the

medium of literature, the pine tree through the fable of the
discontented pine, etc., while recognizing the need of the
human association, fails to note that there is a more straightforward road from mind to the object—direct through connection with life itself; and that the poem and story, the
literary statement, have their place as reinforcements and
idealizations, not as foundation stones. What is wanted, in
other words, is not to fix up a connection of child mind and
nature, but to give free and effective play to the connection
already operating.

2. This suggests at once the practical questions that
are usually discussed under the name of "correlation," questions of such interaction of the various matters studied and
powers under acquisition as will avoid waste, and maintain
unity of mental growth. From the standpoint adopted the
problem is one of differentiation, rather than of correlation
as ordinarily understood. The unity of life, as it presents
itself to the child, binds together and carries along the
different occupations, the diversity of plants, animals, and
geographic conditions; drawing, modelling, games, constructive work, numerical calculations are ways of carrying certain features of it to mental and emotional satisfaction and
completeness. Not much attention is paid in this year to
reading and writing; but it is obvious that if this were regarded as desirable, the same principle would apply. It is
the community and continuity of the subject-matter that
organizes, that correlates; correlation is not through devices
of instruction which the teacher employs in tying together
things in themselves disconnected.

3. Two recognized demands of primary education are
often, at present, not unified, or are even opposed. The need
of the familiar, the already experienced, as a basis for moving upon the unknown and remote, is a commonplace. The
claims of the child's imagination as a factor is at least beginning to be recognized. The problem is to work these two
forces together, instead of separately. The child is too often
given drill upon familiar objects and ideas under the sanc-
tion of the first principle, while he is introduced with equal
directness to the weird, strange, and impossible to satisfy
the claims of the second. The result, it is hardly too much to

say, is a twofold failure. There is no special connection between the unreal, the myth, the fairy tale, and the play of mental imagery. Imagination is not a matter of an impossible subject-matter, but a constructive way of dealing with any subject-matter under the influence of a pervading idea. The point is not to dwell with wearisome iteration upon the familiar and under the guise of object-lessons to keep the senses directed at material which they have already made acquaintance with, but to enliven and illumine the ordinary, commonplace, and homely by using it to build up and appreciate situations previously unrealized and alien. And this also is culture of imagination. Some writers appear to have the impression that the child's imagination has outlet only in myth and fairy tale of ancient time and distant place, or in weaving egregious fabrications regarding sun, moon, and stars; and have even pleaded for a mythical investiture of all "science"—as a way of satisfying the dominating imagination of the child. But fortunately these things are exceptions, are intensifications, are relaxations of the average child; not his pursuits. The John and Jane that most of us know let their imaginations play about the current and familiar contacts and events of life—about father and mother and friend, about steamboats and locomotives, and sheep and cows, about the romance of farm and forest, of seashore and mountain. What is needed, in a word, is to afford occasion by which the child is moved to educe and exchange with others his store of experiences, his range of information, to make new observations correcting and extending them in order to keep his images moving, in order to find mental rest and satisfaction in definite and vivid realization of what is new and enlarging.

With the development of reflective attention come the need and the possibility of a change in the mode of the child's instruction. In the previous paragraphs we have been concerned with the direct, spontaneous attitude that marks the child till into his seventh year—his demand for new experiences, and his desire to complete his partial experiences by building up images and expressing them in play. This attitude is typical of what writers call spontaneous attention, or, as some say, non-voluntary attention.

The child is simply absorbed in what he is doing; the occupation in which he is engaged lays complete hold upon him. He gives himself without reserve. Hence, while there is much energy spent, there is no *conscious* effort; while the child is intent, to the point of engrossment, there is no *conscious* intention.

With the development of a sense of more remote ends, and of the need of directing acts so as to make them means for these ends (a matter discussed in *Middle Works of John Dewey*, 1:226–29), we have the transition to what is termed indirect, or, as some writers prefer to say, voluntary, attention. A result is imaged, and the child attends to what is before him or what he is immediately doing, because it helps to secure the result. Taken by itself, the object or the act might be indifferent or even repulsive. But because it is felt to belong to something desirable or valuable, it borrows the latter's attracting and holding power.

This is the transition to "voluntary" attention, but only the transition. The latter comes fully into being only when the child entertains results in the form of problems or questions, the solution of which he is to seek for himself. In the intervening stage (in the child from eight to, say, eleven or twelve), while the child directs a series of intervening activities on the basis of some end he wishes to reach, this end is something to be done or made, or some tangible result to be reached; the problem is a practical difficulty, rather than an intellectual question. But with growing power, the child can conceive of the end as something to be found out, discovered; and can control his acts and images so as to help in the inquiry and solution. This is reflective attention proper.

In history work there is change from the story and biography form, from discussion of questions that arise, to the formulation of questions. Points about which difference of opinion is possible, matters upon which experience, reflection, etc., can be brought to bear, are always coming up in history. But to use the discussion to develop this matter of doubt and difference into a definite problem, to bring the child to feel just what the difficulty is, and then throw him upon his own resources in looking up material bearing upon the point, and upon his judgment in bringing it to bear, or

getting a solution, is a marked intellectual advance. So in
the science there is a change from the practical attitude of
making and using cameras to the consideration of the problems intellectually involved in this—to principles of light,
angular measurements, etc., which give the theory or explanation of the practice.

In general, this growth is a natural process. But the
proper recognition and use of it is perhaps the most serious
problem in instruction upon the intellectual side. A person
who has gained the power of reflective attention, the power
to hold problems, questions, before the mind, *is* in so far, intellectually speaking, educated. He has mental discipline—
power *of* the mind and *for* the mind. Without this the mind
remains at the mercy of custom and external suggestions.
Some of the difficulties may be barely indicated by referring
to an error that almost dominates instruction of the usual
type. Too often it is assumed that attention can be given
directly to any subject-matter, if only the proper will or disposition be at hand, failure being regarded as a sign of un-
willingness or indocility. Lessons in arithmetic, geography,
and grammar are put before the child, and he is told to
attend in order to learn. But excepting as there is some question, some doubt, present in the mind as a *basis* for this attention, *reflective* attention is impossible. If there is sufficient
intrinsic interest in the material, there will be direct or spontaneous attention, which is excellent so far as it goes, but
which merely of itself does not give power of thought or
internal mental control. If there is not an inherent attracting
power in the material, then (according to his temperament
and training, and the precedents and expectations of the
school) the teacher will either attempt to surround the material with foreign attractiveness, making a bid or offering a
bribe for attention by "making the lesson interesting"; or
else will resort to counterirritants (low marks, threats of non-
promotion, staying after school, personal disapprobation, expressed in a great variety of ways, naggings, continuous calling upon the child to "pay attention," etc.); or, probably, will
use some of both means.

But (1) the attention thus gained is never more than
partial, or divided; and (2) it always remains dependent

upon something external—hence, when the attraction ceases or the pressure lets up, there is little or no gain in inner or intellectual control. And (3) such attention is always for the sake of "learning," *i.e.*, *memorizing ready-made answers to possible questions to be put by another*. True, reflective attention, on the other hand, always involves judging, reasoning, deliberation; it means that the child has a *question of his own*, and is actively engaged in seeking and selecting relevant material with which to answer it, considering the bearings and relations of this material—the kind of solution it calls for. The problem is one's own; hence also the impetus, the stimulus to attention, is one's own; hence also the training secured is one's own—it is discipline, or gain in power of control; that is, a *habit* of considering problems.

It is hardly too much to say that in the traditional education so much stress has been laid upon the presentation to the child of ready-made material (books, object-lessons, teacher's talks, etc.), and the child has been so almost exclusively held to bare responsibility for reciting upon this ready-made material, that there has been only accidental occasion and motive for developing reflective attention. Next to no consideration has been paid to the fundamental necessity —leading the child to realize a problem as his own, so that he is self-induced to attend in order to find out its answer. So completely have the conditions for securing this self-putting of problems been neglected that the very idea of voluntary attention has been radically perverted. It is regarded as measured by unwilling effort—as activity called out by foreign and so repulsive material under conditions of strain, instead of as self-initiated effort. "Voluntary" is treated as meaning the reluctant and disagreeable instead of the free, the self-directed, through personal interest, insight, and power.

9. THE AIM OF HISTORY IN ELEMENTARY EDUCATION

If history be regarded as just the record of the past, it is hard to see any grounds for claiming that it should play any large rôle in the curriculum of elementary education. The past is the past, and the dead may be safely left to bury its dead. There are too many urgent demands in the present, too many calls over the threshold of the future, to permit the child to become deeply immersed in what is forever gone by. Not so when history is considered as an account of the forces and forms of social life. Social life we have always with us; the distinction of past and present is indifferent to it. Whether it was lived just here or just there is a matter of slight moment. It is life for all that; it shows the motives which draw men together and push them apart, and depicts what is desirable and what is hurtful. Whatever history may be for the scientific historian, for the educator it must be an indirect sociology—a study of society which lays bare its process of becoming and its modes of organization. Existing society is both too complex and too close to the child to be studied. He finds no clues into its labyrinth of detail, and can mount no eminence whence to get a perspective of arrangement.

If the aim of historical instruction is to enable the child to appreciate the values of social life, to see in imagination the forces which favor and let men's effective cooperation with one another, to understand the sorts of character that help on and that hold back, the essential thing in its presentation is to make it moving, dynamic. History must be presented not as an accumulation of results or effects, a mere statement of what happened, but as a forceful, acting thing. The motives—that is, the motors—must stand out. To study history is not to amass information, but to use information in constructing a vivid picture of how and why men did thus and so; achieved their successes and came to their failures.

When history is conceived as dynamic, as moving, its economic and industrial aspects are emphasized. These are but technical terms which express the problem with which humanity is unceasingly engaged; how to live, how to master and use nature so as to make it tributary to the enrichment of human life. The great advances in civilization have come through those manifestations of intelligence which have lifted man from his precarious subjection to nature, and revealed to him how he may make its forces cooperate with his own purposes. The social world in which the child now lives is so rich and full that it is not easy to see how much it cost, how much effort and thought lie back of it. Man has a tremendous equipment ready at hand. The child may be led to translate these ready-made resources into fluid terms; he may be led to see man face to face with nature, without inherited capital, without tools, without manufactured materials. And, step by step, he may follow the processes by which man recognized the needs of his situation, thought out the weapons and instruments that enable him to cope with them; and may learn how these new resources opened new horizons of growth and created new problems. The industrial history of man is not a materialistic or merely utilitarian affair. It is a matter of intelligence. Its record is the record of how man learned to think, to think to some effect, to transform the conditions of life so that life itself became a different thing. It is an ethical record as well; the account of the conditions which men have patiently wrought out to serve their ends.

The question of how human beings live, indeed, represents the dominant interest with which the child approaches historic material. It is this point of view which brings those who worked in the past close to the beings with whom he is daily associated, and confers upon him the gift of sympathetic penetration.

The child who is interested in the way in which men lived, the tools they had to do with, the new inventions they made, the transformations of life that arose from the power and leisure thus gained, is eager to repeat like processes in his own action, to remake utensils, to reproduce processes, to rehandle materials. Since he understands their problems and

their successes only by seeing what obstacles and what resources they had from nature, the child is interested in field
and forest, ocean and mountain, plant and animal. By building up a conception of the natural environment in which
lived the people he is studying, he gets his hold upon their
lives. This reproduction he cannot make excepting as he
gains acquaintance with the natural forces and forms with
which he is himself surrounded. The interest in history gives
a more human coloring, a wider significance, to his own
study of nature. His knowledge of nature lends point and
accuracy to his study of history. This is the natural "correlation" of history and science.

This same end, a deepening appreciation of social life,
decides the place of the biographic element in historical
instruction. That historical material appeals to the child most
completely and vividly when presented in individual form,
when summed up in the lives and deeds of some heroic
character, there can be no doubt. Yet it is possible to use
biographies so that they become a collection of mere stories,
interesting, possibly, to the point of sensationalism, but yet
bringing the child no nearer to comprehension of social life.
This happens when the individual who is the hero of the tale
is isolated from his social environment; when the child is not
brought to feel the social situations which evoked his acts and
the social progress to which his deeds contributed. If biography is presented as a dramatic summary of social needs
and achievements, if the child's imagination pictures the
social defects and problems that clamored for the man and
the ways in which the individual met the emergency, then
the biography is an organ of social study.

A consciousness of the social aim of history prevents
any tendency to swamp history in myth, fairy story, and
merely literary renderings. I cannot avoid the feeling that
much as the Herbartian school has done to enrich the elementary curriculum in the direction of history, it has often
inverted the true relationship existing between history and
literature. In a certain sense the *motif* of American colonial
history and of De Foe's *Robinson Crusoe* are the same. Both
represent man who has achieved civilization, who has at-
tained a certain maturity of thought; who has developed

ideals and means of action, but is suddenly thrown back upon his own resources, having to cope with a raw and often hostile nature, and to regain success by sheer intelligence, energy, and persistence of character. But when *Robinson Crusoe* supplies the material for the curriculum of the third- or fourth-grade child, are we not putting the cart before the horse? Why not give the child the reality with its much larger sweep, its intenser forces, its more vivid and lasting value for life, using the *Robinson Crusoe* as an imaginative idealization in a particular case of the same sort of problems and activities? Again, whatever may be the worth of the study of savage life in general, and of the North American Indians in particular, why should that be approached circuitously through the medium of *Hiawatha*, instead of at first hand, employing indeed the poem to furnish the idealized and culminating touches to a series of conditions and struggles which the child has previously realized in more specific form? Either the life of the Indian presents some permanent questions and factors in social life, or it has next to no place in a scheme of instruction. If it has such a value, this should be made to stand out on its own account, instead of being lost in the very refinement and beauty of a purely literary presentation.

The same end, the understanding of character and social relations in their natural dependence, enables us, I think, to decide upon the importance to be attached to chronological order in historical instruction. Considerable stress has of late been laid upon the supposed necessity of following the development of civilization through the successive steps in which it actually took place—beginning with the valleys of the Euphrates and the Nile, and coming on down through Greece, Rome, etc. The point urged is that the present depends upon the past, and each phase of the past upon a prior past.

We are here introduced to a conflict between the logical and psychological interpretation of history. If the aim be an appreciation of what social life is and how it goes on, then, certainly, the child must deal with what is near in spirit, not with the remote. The difficulty with the Babylonian or Egyptian life is not so much its remoteness in time, as its remoteness from the present interests and aims of social life. It does not simplify enough and does not generalize enough; or, at least, it does not do so in the right way. It does it by omission of what is significant now, rather than by presenting these factors arranged on a lower scale. Its salient features are hard to get at and to understand, even by the specialist. It undoubtedly presents factors which contributed to later life, and which modified the course of events in the stream of time. But the child has not arrived at a point where he can appreciate abstract causes and specialized contributions. What he needs is a picture of typical relations, conditions, and activities. In this respect, there is much of pre-historic life which is much closer to him than the complicated and artificial life of Babylon or of Egypt. When a child is capable of appreciating institutions, he is capable of seeing what special institutional idea each historic nation stands for, and what factor it has contributed to the present complex of institutions. But this period arrives only when the child is beginning to be capable of abstracting causes in other realms as well; in other words, when he is approaching the time of secondary education.

In this general scheme three periods or phases are recognized: first comes the generalized and simplified history—history which is hardly history at all in the local or chronological sense, but which aims at giving the child insight into, and sympathy with, a variety of social activities. This period includes the work of the six-year-old children in studying typical occupations of people in the country and city at present; of the seven-year-old children in working out the evolution of inventions and their effects upon life, and of the eight-year-old children in dealing with the great movements of migration, exploration, and discovery which have brought the whole round world into human ken. The work of the first two years is evidently quite independent of any particular people or any particular person—that is, of historical data in the strict sense of the term. At the same time, plenty of scope is provided through dramatization for the introduction of the individual factor. The account of the great explorers and the discoverers serves to make the transition to what is local and specific, that which depends upon certain specified persons who lived at certain specified places and times.

This introduces us to the second period where local conditions and the definite activities of particular bodies of people become prominent—corresponding to the child's growth in power of dealing with limited and positive fact. Since Chicago, since the United States, are localities with which the child can, by the nature of the case, most effectively deal, the material of the next three years is derived directly and indirectly from this source. Here, again, the third year is a transitional year, taking up the connections of American life with European. By this time the child should be ready to deal not with social life in general, or even with the social life with which he is most familiar, but with certain thoroughly differentiated and, so to speak, peculiar types of social life; with the special significance of each and the particular contribution it has made to the whole world history. Accordingly, in the next period the chronological order is followed, beginning with the ancient world about the Mediterranean and coming down again through European history to the peculiar and differentiating factors of American history.

The program is not presented as the only one meeting the problem, but as a contribution, the outcome not of thought but of considerable experimenting and shifting of subjects from year to year, to the problem of giving material which takes vital hold upon the child and at the same time leads on, step by step, to more thorough and accurate knowledge of both the principles and facts of social life, and makes a preparation for later specialized historic studies.

Index

INDEX

Arithmetic: as taught in school, not related to child's life, 47

Arnold, Matthew: on uniformity of education in France, 23

Art: graphic, in school, 52–53; synthesis of, with science and industry, 54

Art instinct: of child, defined, 29–30

Attention: spontaneous, defined, 100–101; voluntary, defined, 101; reflective, defined, 102–3

Biography: as an organ of social study, 106–7

Carpentry: as introduction to physics, 51

Child: as centre of new education, 21–24

Columbia University Teachers College: training of teachers at, 55–56

Communication instinct: of child, defined, 29

Constructive impulse: of child, defined, 29

Cooking: as introduction to science, 50–51

De Foe, Daniel: *Robinson Crusoe* discussed, 106–7

Discipline: change in, necessity of larger social evolution, 11–12; philosophy of, at University Elementary School, 65–66

Education: available to all as result of industrial revolution, 16–17; controlled by specialized aims, 18; traditional, based on uniformity, 21–23; waste of human life in, 39

Froebel, Friedrich Wilhelm: educational principles of, 81–85; his *Mother Play* discussed, 83–84; symbolism of, 84–85

Games: use of, in University Elementary School, 82–84

Geography: unity of all sciences found in, 13

Grammar school: origin of, 42

Growth: stages of, in child, related to education, 73–80

Hiawatha: related to social study, 107

History: as taught in University Elementary School, 62–63; American, 63; Greek and Roman, 63; American, related to growth stage of child, 74–75; use of, in elementary education, 104–9; periods of, related to child's stages of development, 108–9

Home life: used as subject-matter in kindergarten, 87–88

Household: as centre of industrial occupation, 7;